PRAYERS OF POWER

A 40-Day Journal

Mark Doss and Amy Jo Wrobel

WESTBOW
PRESS®
A DIVISION OF THOMAS NELSON
& ZONDERVAN

WestBow Press books may be ordered through booksellers or by contacting:

WestBow Press
A Division of Thomas Nelson & Zondervan
1663 Liberty Drive
Bloomington, IN 47403
www.westbowpress.com
844-714-3454

Interior Graphics/Art Credit: Keelia Paulson

ISBN: 978-1-6642-8836-2 (sc)
ISBN: 978-1-6642-8837-9 (hc)
ISBN: 978-1-6642-8835-5 (e)

Print information available on the last page.

WestBow Press rev. date: 01/09/2023

Contents

Foreword

By: Gov. Kim Reynolds

Prayer has always been an essential part of my life. For many years, I've have made a point to begin each day with a morning devotion or a passage from Scripture that grounds me in God's Word. It reminds me not to rely on myself but only on His sustaining grace, no matter what comes.

And plenty of hardships have come Iowa's way while I've been in office (the worst days of the pandemic come to mind). So I put a lot of pressure on myself to deliver for the people I serve, and without turning to God and trusting in His Providence, it would surely be too much for me.

It's not just my own prayers, either. During the pandemic, for example, I received a steady stream of notes from Iowans assuring me that they were lifting me up in prayer, asking the Lord to bless me with wisdom and resolve. I treasure the letters, but I'm even more grateful for the prayers. I needed them then, and I need them today.

In other words, my own experience has corroborated the words of St. Paul: "The Lord is at hand; do not be anxious about anything, but in everything by prayer and supplication with thanksgiving let your requests be made known to God. And the peace of God, which surpasses all understanding, will guard your hearts and minds in Christ Jesus."

In Prayers of Power, the wonderful people at the Iowa Prayer Breakfast draw out the lessons of Scripture to help make the peace "which surpasses all understanding" available to us all. I can't wait to get started, and I hope you'll join me.

Preface

By N. Joel Fry

What a joy and privilege it is to be a part of the Iowa Prayer Breakfast! This year I have the distinct honor of serving as the 2023 Prayer Breakfast Committee Chairman. As a State Representative in the Iowa House of Representatives, my family and I have time and again experienced first-hand the power of prayer through the Iowa Prayer Breakfast and its mission.

"The Iowa Prayer Breakfast exists to glorify Jesus Christ through the public affirmation of His sovereignty over our State and our Nation. In obedience to 2 Chronicles 7:14, we pray for God's intervention in the affairs of our State and His favor and blessing on our leaders." For over 60 years Iowans from across the State have gathered on Maundy Thursday to glorify our Risen Savior Jesus Christ through Prayer, Scripture, Worship, and inspiring faith-filled messages. We pray for blessings over the leaders of our State and Nation in one voice before the Lord Jesus Christ.

Started in 1961 by Des Moines Mayor Reinhold Carlson, the Iowa Prayer Breakfast still today remains focused on beginning the Easter weekend with a focus on prayers for our State and Nation. May we never take for granted the great freedoms born from a sovereign God and the sacrifice of many who followed Him ahead of us. With great enthusiasm and encouragement, I invite you to join me on this journey of prayer and devotion as we share in the Prayers of Power. Once again joining together in one spirit for the leaders of our great State and Nation, we will continue to find forgiveness for our sins and experience the healing hands of God on our land.

May the Lord Almighty richly bless you and your family this Easter season!

N. Joel Fry

Introduction

Prayers of Power is a devotional prayer journal that illuminates some of the Bible's examples of how God used ordinary people serving in positions of power and the lessons they learned from prayer. Corporately and individually, we have much to learn in our spiritual journeys about prayer. The Iowa Prayer Breakfast Committee desires this book to be a valuable tool in your daily walk with God, increasing your desire for worship through prayer and your effectiveness in praying. Read the highlighted Scripture passage, real-life stories, and personal applications our authors have written. The journaling pages offer space to record thoughts and ideas you want to implement in your life. Write out your prayer-filled requests, thanksgiving, and words as another form of worship. We desire that the Spirit of God uses Prayers of Power as a beautifully written instrument of praise and prayer in your quiet time communing with God.

We encourage you to take the challenge of deepening your prayer life through these 40 devotionals, individually or with a group. Let the Spirit of God guide and direct you through this book, deepening your relationship with God. Our challenge to you is to prayerfully and powerfully ask our Lord Jesus Christ to teach you to pray, regardless of whether you are a new or veteran follower of Him! The Iowa Prayer Breakfast Committee's prayer for you is that you will find your prayers resulting in "great power that produces wonderful results!" (James 5:16 NLT).

Confess your sins to each other and pray for each other so that you may be healed. The earnest prayer of a righteous person has great power and produces wonderful results. Elijah was as human as we are, yet when he prayed earnestly that no rain would fall, none fell for three and a half years! Then, when he prayed again, the sky sent down rain, and the earth began to yield its crops (James 5:16-18, NLT).

Day 1

God is our Dwelling Place

Psalm 90:1-17

"Lord, you have been our dwelling place in
all generations" (Psalm 90:1, ESV).

"There is a God, and you are not Him." I love catchy phrases, and I remember seeing this one on a T-shirt several years ago. I think the reason it caught my interest is the reminder that, too often, we try to play God in our lives and the lives of others without success. Every one of us needs a reminder that we cannot play the role that belongs to God alone. Psalm 90 expresses a tension of life: God created us for eternity with Him, but we are caught in the temporal world and frustrated with our inability to access eternity. Our answer is to act like God or to replace Him with ourselves or our idols. The result is absolute failure and frustration. God's answer is to find our home in Him and satisfy our needs with His loving favor. Augustine of Hippo has perhaps stated it best: "Thou hast made us for thyself, O Lord, and our heart is restless until it finds its rest in thee."

God is eternal, and we are not. Psalm 90 says God is from eternity to eternity. God is sovereign, and we are not. God is the Lord of the universe and the One to whom everyone is accountable. That is the problem. God created us to be in a relationship with Him forever. He desires to be our refuge and for us to be perfectly connected and at home with Him. But our rebellious hearts make it impossible. God instead becomes our Judge, and His anger pushes us away. Rather than enjoying the eternal relationship, we experience rejection, pain, sorrow, and the restlessness described by Augustine's quote, reminding us that we are restless until we rest in God. Our temporary life underscores the infinite distance between God and us. Thus, we are continually frustrated by our inability to access the beauty of God's forever nature. According to Psalm 90, life is filled with toil and trouble, discouraging us and robbing us of our joy. The experience of life is indeed brief and painful.

So, why should we pray, and what should we pray? Psalm 90 is titled "A Psalm of Moses." Moses is the leader who guides the children of Israel out of Egypt, and he is the one who presents the holy law of God to the Israelites. His knowledge of God's eternal nature and justice leads him to teach us that God has a right to be angry with us because of our rebellion. But he also admits that while deserving of God's judgment, God does not want anyone to remain frustrated and alienated from God. Moses' prayer seeks a solution. "So teach us to number our days so we may get a heart of wisdom" (v.12, ESV). Our prayer might be phrased as follows: "Eternal God, help us to understand our finiteness and that we are prone to run away from You. Grant us wisdom to trust You and come home to You."

Additionally, this prayer of Moses guides us to ask for the mercy and forgiveness that will restore our relationship with God. We may continue our prayer, "God, please forgive our Running from You and granting us satisfaction based on Your unfailing and eternal love. Please give us gladness for all our days to replace the toil and trouble that invades our lives. And please show us that You are present in our lives. Lord God, we ask You to grant us success based on Your gracious favor. Let us come home to You and 'establish the work of our hands!' (v. 17, ESV). On this side of the New Testament, we have the vantage point of understanding this opportunity to come home to our Eternal God is possible because of the sacrifice of our Lord Jesus Christ. Jesus invites us to "Come to me, all who labor and are heavy laden, and I will give you rest" (Matthew 11:35, ESV). The book of Hebrews also invites us: "Let us then with confidence draw near to the throne of grace, that we may receive mercy and find grace to help in time of need" (Hebrews 4:16, ESV). From this Psalm of Moses and these two New Testament invitations, we learn the power of prayers that help us run to the Eternal God for mercy and grace. We can find the good in coming home to the Lord our God and resting in His eternal, unfailing love! MPD

date

scripture

PRAISE
& THANKS

PRAYERS FOR MY

CHURCH

FAMILY&FRIENDS

NATION&WORLD

ON MY **HEART** TODAY

Day 2

God Will Do Right

Genesis 18:22-33

"Shall not the Judge of all the earth do what
is just?" (Genesis 18:25, ESV).

We need to talk! Not to go negative immediately, but that statement usually signals trouble and a conversation I want to avoid. It is not a good sign when a spouse, a boss, or a friend tells you that "we need to talk." This Bible passage in Genesis 18 presents God concluding that He needed to talk with Abraham. The Bible author uses what is termed anthropomorphism. God is described in human terms as preparing to speak with another human. The dialogue between God and Abraham becomes quite interesting when Abraham finds out about God's upcoming plans. God is making a holy and righteous decision to destroy the cities of Sodom and Gomorrah because of their great sin. Abraham responds to God with the argument that He is merciful and gracious. If there are righteous people in these cities, then it would be wrong for God to destroy them.

Abraham continues to bargain with God. First, he acknowledges the righteous judgments of God. "Shall not the Judge of all the earth do what is just?" (Genesis 18:25, ESV). Our human wisdom says that negotiation should begin with respect for the other person. So, Abraham showed respect for God, the Righteous Judge, which we should imitate in our prayers.

Regarding prayer, some people think that they cannot say anything that challenges God. Others feel they can speak to God any way they please and tell him like it is. Both approaches are wrong. Abraham guides us in the power of prayer by helping us realize that God is ready for us to converse with Him, an honest and challenging conversation if we respect His righteousness and holy standing. Disrespecting God is unfruitful and sinful. Not being honest with God is also unfruitful and sinful.

Taking this respect further, Abraham recognized God's right to judge these cities for their sinful rebellion. If God is the Judge of all the earth, it is His call when and how to pronounce judgment. Not to take us too far away from the main subject of prayer, but some will resist hearing this story because of the kinds of sin that caused God to decide the punishment for these cities was necessary. Please refrain from running from the lessons we can learn in this story. Note the city's residents were openly rebellious against God. Amid this rebellion, God heard the cries of the victims being hurt by the citizens' rebellious actions. God is always the God of the weak and the hurting. He will act to protect those who are vulnerable.

There is an interesting verse in Ezekiel that describes the sin of Sodom and Gomorrah. "Behold, this was the guilt of your sister Sodom: she and her daughters had pride, excess of food, and prosperous ease but did not aid the poor and needy. They were haughty and did an abomination before me. So I removed them when I saw it" (Ezekiel 16:49, ESV). Yes, in Genesis 19, as Lot hosts the angelic visitors, the sexual advances of the people are rejected by Lot. But the city's residents were guilty of more than this because they, in their abundance, failed to care for the poor and needy. No matter the list of sins before a holy and righteous God, we must all recognize that we have sinned and fallen short of God's glory. Because of that, death is what we face. We may debate the list of wrongs that God defines, but may He give us the grace to see wrong as He does. Every person has this judgment of God facing us. We are not good enough to be in a relationship with God. Our list of sins may differ from another person's, and each person will struggle with certain sins more than others. But learning to pray powerfully leads us to finally give in to the right that God is the final determiner of right and wrong, and we must listen for His judgments.

Powerful praying also wrestles to understand God's character, which is righteous and gracious. On the one hand, God is perfectly righteous and demands that we are perfect with no wrongdoing. On the other hand, God is perfectly merciful and ready to grant us forgiveness. Back to Abraham and his conversation with God. Abraham presented the side of grace back to God. If God cares about the vulnerable and the righteous, He cannot destroy them along with the guilty. Abraham asked God to save the cities if there were fifty righteous people. Not sure if there were fifty, Abraham lowered his numbers until he finally asked God if he would spare the cities if there were ten righteous. God agreed! We later learn there were not ten righteous people in the city, so God proceeded with a judgment that destroyed the city of Sodom (and Gomorrah). I remember hearing others discuss the idea that prayer is not getting God to agree with us but getting us to agree with God. That is the beauty of this prayer conversation that Abraham had with God. God acknowledged Abraham's desires and decided to protect the righteous, but God had to act with righteous judgment, and Abraham had to submit to the decision of God. "Shall not the Judge of all the earth do what is just?" (Genesis 18:25, ESV).

God's character and judgments will always be a mystery to us. Still, He is willing for us to talk with Him and wrestle with His holiness and grace until we can leave the final decision with God and trust Him with the outcomes. That is powerful praying. I said I did not want to run to the negative too quickly with that statement, "we need to talk." The beauty of a relationship with your spouse, a child, a parent, or a friend is when you no longer fear the statement but welcome it. We need to talk becomes the best invitation to engage in an honest conversation with this person you love and respect. This kind of prayer with God can also become a welcome and powerful opportunity. God, we need to talk. I need you to help me understand, and if I am unable to understand fully, allow me to continue with confidence that You ultimately know what is best and will do what is right. MPD

date

scripture

PRAISE & THANKS

PRAYERS FOR MY

CHURCH

FAMILY&FRIENDS

NATION&WORLD

ON MY **HEART** TODAY

Day 3

Please Deliver Me

Genesis 32:9-12

"I am not worthy of the least of all the deeds of steadfast
love and all the faithfulness that you have shown
to your servant…." (Genesis 32:10, ESV).

"We are not worthy! We are not worthy!" Were you like my friends and
me, who would mockingly bow and cry out these words when someone
acted like they were better, wiser, or more important than the others in
the group? In this Bible story, we see Jacob crying to God, "I am not
worthy," but it was not in jest. He was sincere because he was scared to
face his brother, Esau. Jacob, the grandson of Abraham, just left his father-
in-law, Laban, after a battle to save his family from Laban's wrath. Then,
returning to his grandfather's homeland, he knew he had to face Esau.
His only and best hope was calling on the God of Abraham and Isaac to
help. With complete humility, Jacob confesses his unworthiness and his
need for deliverance.

Why would he fear Esau? Jacob's history has him cheating and stealing
the family blessing from his older brother, Esau. Esau and Jacob were
twins, but Esau was the first out of the womb, so he was the one who
should have received his father's blessing. Through lying and deceit, Jacob
and his mother stole the birthright from Isaac and left Esau without this
blessing due to the firstborn son. God had directed Jacob to return to

his homeland, which meant he would have to deal with Esau. Jacob sent messengers to Esau asking to have favor on him with a reunion that would overlook their strained relationship. The messengers came back to tell Jacob that Esau was coming to meet him. You can feel the storyline escalate as Jacob imagines the worst. Esau is coming to battle him and harm his family. From the struggle with Laban and an uneasy truce to dealing with Esau, Jacob was scared and knew he needed God's help.

Jacob has always been a challenging character in the Bible for me. He was a schemer and conniver and a cheat. The theft with his mother was just the first of Jacob's wicked stunts. To be fair, he was also very resourceful and entrepreneurial. God's resources caused Jacob to flourish while living with his future father-in-law. We can also acknowledge that the Bible shows Jacob was the recipient of lying and cheating. Laban promised his daughter, Rachel, to Jacob in marriage and then deceived him on the wedding night by placing Leah in Rachel's place. So why would God even bother with a guy who is so dishonorable? God's mercy and grace are offered to us, even a guy like Jacob. We are not worthy, yet God shows His mercy and grace to each of us!

Additionally, there was a promise or covenant in play. God promised Abraham that He would bless him, and Jacob was in line to be the person through whom God would make good on His covenant promise. While God was working as He promised, something was also happening to Jacob. Through God's patient guidance, Jacob learned that He required God's deliverance and to live his life according to God's plans and purposes. This brings us to the lessons for powerful praying that we can learn from Jacob. First, Jacob was humbled, and in humility, he called upon God for help and deliverance. Life has a way of wearing us down. We can give up or become cynical or cruel. We will often choose to pay back evil to others just like they have treated us. But you and I can discover the God who cares, loves, and seeks to bring us under His blessing. Through God's kindness, we can dismiss the need for revenge. After leaving Laban, the Bible tells us that "Jacob went on his way, and the angels of God met him" (Genesis 32:1, ESV). God was helping Jacob to see His better ways, and Jacob was now ready to claim the promises of God. "But you said, 'I will surely do you good, and make your offspring as the sand of the seas which cannot be numbered for multitude'" (Genesis 32:12, ESV). God delights to have us pray back His words to Him. Remembering the word of God, allowing it to invade our hearts and minds as we meditate on it, and then telling God that we remember what He promised is good for us to do. It helps us to pray powerfully as we rehearse the promises of God.

Jacob, later renamed Israel by God, teaches us an important lesson. It is possible to scheme and manipulate and even be successful in living that way. But the more incredible opportunity is to lay down our schemes and humbly claim the promises of God. I am reminded of the old familiar hymn, "I need Thee, oh, I need Thee; Ev'ry hour I need Thee; Oh, bless me now, my Savior, I come to Thee."

We may choose to pray, Heavenly Father; you have promised in Hebrews 13:4 that "I will never leave you nor forsake you" (ESV). Thank you for that promise and that gift. I need you, Lord Jesus! You promised in John 16:33, "Peace I leave with you; my peace I give to you. Not as the world gives do I give to you. Let not your hearts be troubled, neither let them be afraid" (ESV). I need your peace! I am not worthy of your love and faithfulness, but I need you. So, help me, Lord God, and deliver me! MPD

date

scripture

PRAISE
&THANKS

PRAYERS FOR MY

CHURCH

FAMILY&FRIENDS

NATION&WORLD

ON MY **HEART TODAY**

Day 4

Wrestling with God

Genesis 32:22-33

"And Jacob was left alone. And a man wrestled
with him until the breaking of the day."
(Genesis 32:25, ESV).

I did not sleep well last night. I had these wild dreams, and they felt so real! Too often, my wife and I will have these conversations as we wake up in the morning and confess to each other that we are tired and not ready to face the day. The story in Genesis 32 tells us that Jacob had a bad dream. Well, it was more than a dream. It was a meeting with God and a wrestling match between God and man. At the risk of rushing to the end of the story, it was a match where both won. God redeemed Jacob, and Jacob received the blessing of God. Yesterday's look at Jacob saw how he claimed the promises of God and called on God to deliver him. Today, we see Jacob preparing to meet Esau by dividing his flocks and servants so he could offer Esau gifts to appease him. After these preparations, Jacob helped his family cross the river stream, and he stayed behind alone. God had an essential next step for Jacob.

God was ready to deliver Jacob because of His promises to Abraham, but God needed to change Jacob. The name change from Jacob to Israel signifies this change. The change would come as God wrestled with Jacob. We have identified Jacob as a schemer. He asked God to deliver him, but he still divided his assets and prepared for the best he could imagine. God wanted to move beyond Jacob's best to God's best. Why do we scheme and plan and act as if we are the ones who will succeed or fail without allowing God to be involved? You might say this story is not a prayer because Jacob wasn't going to God. God was coming to him. But I would argue that the prayer experience comes when Jacob and God talk during the wrestling match. But allow me to back up just a little bit. In the wrestling match, Jacob was doing okay in this wrestling match. He was determined to win and used all his strength to do so. Finally, "the man," or the one Jacob will realize is God resorts to a power play of crippling Jacob's thigh. God brought Jacob to the end of his strength and schemes.

Something happened to Jacob beyond a physical injury. Through God's wrestling, Jacob finally realized that the promises of God would be his deliverance. Rather than depending on himself and his best efforts, he realized that he could only survive with God's blessing. Jacob held onto "the man" and would not let him go until he committed to blessing Jacob. Powerful prayers occur when we wrestle with God and finally come to the place where we acknowledge our schemes and reliance on ourselves are not enough. We cannot get to where we want to go without God's mighty work in our lives. Jacob saw the future, and the obstacles were too significant for him to overcome. He finally let go of the blessing he stole from Esau and asked God to give him the blessing he needed but did not deserve. God granted the blessing as He changed Jacob's name to Israel. The new name demonstrated the authority of God over Jacob and showed that Jacob was now facing his future in the power and promises of God. The blessings promised to his grandfather and father and directly to him are given as God's gracious gift.

Recognizing our limitations and our need for God is where we need to arrive. We need God to overcome the forces that will destroy us and the better future and promises He desires to give us. Expressing our need for God and asking for His help is a powerful prayer. We no longer depend on ourselves for our destiny but trust God with our life and future. Our prayer of faith accesses the promise of life and deliverance that only God can give.

The Apostle Paul describes it this way: "But God, being rich in mercy, because of the great love with which he loved us, even when we were dead in our trespasses, made us alive together with Christ—by grace, you have been saved— and raised us with him and seated us with him in the heavenly places in Christ Jesus, so that in the coming ages he might show the immeasurable riches of his grace in kindness toward us in Christ Jesus" (Ephesians 2:4-7, ESV).

We can choose to pray like this: Jesus, I cannot gain the life I need and desire apart from You. But, by faith and because of your grace, I receive this life and ask You, the Lord Jesus Christ, to become my deliverer and my salvation. I have struggled and now rest in the blessing of life that comes from You alone. With a thankful heart, I receive your gracious gift in the name of Jesus. Amen. That is a powerful prayer! MPD

date

scripture

PRAISE
& THANKS

PRAYERS FOR MY

CHURCH

FAMILY&FRIENDS

NATION&WORLD

ON MY **HEART** TODAY

Day 5

No One Can Stand In Guilt Before God

Ezra 9:5-15 HCSB

"Lord, God of Israel, You are righteous, for we survive as a remnant today. Here we are before You with our guilt, though no one can stand in Your presence because of this." Ezra 9:15 HSCB

A remnant of Israelites had been allowed to return to Jerusalem after long captivity in Babylon. God had called Ezra to minister to the needs of this group of people. Upon their arrival, a time of sacrifice and worship began at the restored temple. Soon, the leaders brought Ezra a report that sin had infiltrated the people of Israel, religious leaders, and Levites. Corruption pervaded all three levels of the community.

Ezra, appalled by the report, immediately began to mourn, tearing his tunic and robe and pulling out the hair on his head and beard. A sign of great grief and remorse, Ezra was utterly devastated.

Sitting in front of the temple, Ezra began to pray as others slowly gathered around him. The people who trembled at the words of the God of Israel now stood around the praying prophet, grieving over the nation's sin. Then, as the evening offering begins, Ezra stands and begins to cry out to God in prayer.

Erza became the mediator on behalf of the remnant who had allowed the vile abominations of surrounding nations to influence not only Israel but God's law and instructed them to have nothing to do with them. What would have grieved previous generations had become commonplace among the people. No wonder Ezra's prayer of confession declared, "Here we are before You with our guilt, though no one can stand in Your presence because of this." (v. 15b)

Psalm 130:3 says, "If You considered sins, Lord, who could stand?" Perhaps the psalmist remembered this time in Israel's history. All would be lost if this was the verdict of each sinner. Guilty before God. Not one of us could stand. No excuse would suffice. The psalmist continues in verse 4, "But with You, there is forgiveness so that You may be revered." The Lord's compassion offers us grace and mercy through His forgiveness when we humble our hearts before Him.

In Matthew 3:3, another prophet, John the Baptist, came preaching, saying, "Repent, because the kingdom of heaven has come near!" The time had come for Christ to be revealed to a sinful world. Ezra brought the people to the temple before a Holy God. Christ, the embodiment of the temple, brings an evil world to Himself. The perfect atonement of Christ now offers forgiveness to the repentant. We were found guilty, but Christ, our advocate, declared us "not guilty." Standing in the courtroom with God as judge, would He declare you "guilty" or "forgiven"?

How are you affected by the sin of others? Does it grieve your heart, or are you numb to the "filthiness" of the world around you?

Pray for your "remnant," your town, church, and family as Ezra prayed, "Our guilt is as high as the heavens. Grace has come from You, Lord, to preserve us. Lord God of Israel, You are righteous, for we survive as a remnant today. God gives us new life and light to our eyes." AJW

date *scripture*

PRAISE & THANKS

PRAYERS FOR MY

CHURCH

FAMILY&FRIENDS

NATION&WORLD

ON MY HEART TODAY

Day 6

Salvation Belongs to the Lord

Jonah 2:1-9

"I will sacrifice to You with a voice of thanksgiving. I will
fulfill what I have vowed. Salvation is from the Lord."
Jonah 2:9 HCSB

Have you ever been told to do something and chose not to do it? We are all guilty of willful disobedience. I learned this very well when I taught 4-year-old children in a preschool. When confronted with their disobedience, some children would run and hide; other times, they immediately repented. But occasionally, I faced a very strong-willed child who would, in defiance, look at me, perpetrate his crime, and then run in a different direction from where I was standing. Discipline was necessary and immediate.

In the book of Jonah, we read about another individual who, much like the 4-year-olds I taught, deliberately disobeyed God's command. God had selected Jonah to deliver a message of repentance to the city of Nineveh. Rather than obey what God instructed him to do, Jonah ran in the opposite direction. The Ninevites were wicked evil people over 500 miles away from where Jonah lived, so trying to run from the presence of the Lord, Jonah went in the opposite direction, boarding a ship that was sailing away from Nineveh.

Jonah thought he'd hide away on a cargo ship, trying to out-maneuver God, but God sent a violent storm to get his attention. Instead, the ship's crew realized that Jonah was the cause of their impending doom and threw him overboard to appease God's judgment. In their reverent fear of the God of the Hebrews, they made vows and sacrifices to God. Then, over the side of the boat went Jonah.

God wasn't finished with Jonah. Now, both Jonah and Nineveh needed to repent. God miraculously provided a great fish to swallow Jonah, and it was here that he experienced a three-day stay in the belly of the fish. Jonah's rebellion and God's discipline brought Jonah to the point of humble repentance. Jonah realized that God had graciously spared his life. First and foremost, Jonah "called to the Lord in his distress."

When we find ourselves in a place of distress, sometimes of our own making, we try to fix things in our sufficiency; however, there are times when we have no place to turn but up. So our immediate response should be to look up and call out to God as our redeemer and deliverer. As he cries for help, Jonah acknowledges God's discipline for his disobedience and promise of deliverance in distress.

"Jonah couldn't save himself, and nobody on earth could save him, but the Lord could do it, for "salvation is of the Lord!" (Wiersbe, The Bible Exposition Commentary-Old Testament The Prophets, p. 381). God is faithful and true, fulfilling His vows to His children. When God asks us to do something, let us remember His promises and salvation, and follow Him in obedience, wherever He asks us to go. AJW

Can you think of a time when you ran from God? How did it turn out?

What was the result if you repented and did what God called you to do?

How has it affected your walk with the Lord if you disobey Him?

date | *scripture*

PRAISE & THANKS

PRAYERS FOR MY

CHURCH

FAMILY&FRIENDS

NATION&WORLD

ON MY **HEART** TODAY

Day 7

Be Merciful to Me, a Sinner

Luke 18:9-14

"Everyone who exalts himself will be humbled, but the one
who humbles himself will be exalted." Luke 18:14 HCSB

We were sitting in a Bible study with five other couples. Part of our study
that day led us to a time of confession and repentance of sinful behavior
we were holding onto that might be keeping us at arm's length in our
relationship with God. As we went around the circle, tears coursed down
our faces as we humbled ourselves before each other and God. Finally,
it was the last couple's turn to share. The woman took a deep breath,
sat straight up in her chair, and declared, "I have nothing to confess.
I'm thankful to God that I have led a pure and holy life and have done
nothing wrong." One of the group members said, "Then I suggest you
check your pride at the door. Otherwise, you have no place here. It's just
for us sinners."

This scene has played an enormous part in my life since that moment
over 20 years ago. God calls it to my remembrance when I get a little
"puffed up" with pride and my self-righteous tendencies. Maybe that's why
Jesus taught His disciples the Parable of the Pharisee and the Tax Collector.
But, unlike room settings, Jesus often taught His disciples as they walked
and sat out in the open. During this particular time of teaching, a group
of Pharisees joined them (Luke 17:20).

Pharisees were a group of highly educated scholars who wore their piety of devoutness and religiosity as a badge of honor. They openly prayed loudly in the streets and temple and frequently fasted, drawing attention to themselves. They studied God's law, exercising their knowledge many times, challenging Jesus repeatedly through His earthly ministry. Their one glaring sin was that of pride.[2] "The Pharisee took his stand and was praying like this: God, I thank You that I'm not like other people-greedy, unrighteous, adulterers, or even like this tax collector. I fast twice a week; I give a tenth of everything I get." (vv. 11-12)

Standing off in the corner was the tax collector. This man, known for his extortion, working on behalf of the Roman government, and excising taxes from his fellow citizens at exorbitant rates, was unliked by society. Through Jesus' ministry, He often ate and socialized with this group of men synonymously coupled with "sinners," even choosing a tax collector for one of His disciples. (Luke 5:29-31).

The tax collector was overcome with sin, refusing to lift his eyes to heaven. Instead, he beat his chest with great remorse and grief, begging God to forgive him. In a brief prayer of repentance, Jesus told His disciples and the listening group of Pharisees that this one, this despicable tax collector, went away justified, but not the Pharisees. The tax collector's humility of spirit was beautiful to God. "Jesus replied to them: I have not come to call the righteous, but sinners to repentance" (Luke 5:31). AJW

Thoughts of Reflection

Are you filled with self-righteousness like the Pharisee or humility of spirit like the tax collector?

Humble yourself in quiet prayer, asking God to reveal the answer to you.

Write a prayer of confession and thanksgiving for the gift of forgiveness through Jesus Christ.

[2] (https://www.britannica.com/topic/Pharisee)

date

scripture

PRAISE
&THANKS

PRAYERS FOR MY

CHURCH

FAMILY&FRIENDS

NATION&WORLD

ON MY HEART TODAY

Day 8

Help My Unbelief

Mark 9:14-29

"I do believe! Help my unbelief." Mark 9:24 HCSB

The father of the epileptic son was desperate for his beloved male child to be healed from the convulsions that threatened to cause physical damage. From birth, this child suffered from debilitating seizures made worse by the evil intentions of the demons inside him. Approaching the disciples, the father begged them to heal his son; much to their embarrassment, they could not cast out the demons.

Jesus, Peter, James, and John were returning from the Mount of Transfiguration when the crowd caught sight of Him. Immediately, the entire group was amazed and ran to greet Him. Then, caught up in the multitude of people, the father answered Jesus' query regarding the scribes and His disciples' disputation. "Teacher, I brought my Son to You."

Have you ever expected to see someone of authority only to be greeted by an underling who could not fulfill your request? I'm sure the father was more than disappointed and perhaps a little frustrated. The child's condition had continued to worsen, and the father was at the end of his rope.

When Jesus found out His disciples could not cast out the demon, He cried out in exasperation, "You unbelieving generation! How long will I be with you? How long must I put up with you?" Jesus had given all power and authority to the disciples (Mark 3:15, 6:7). Yet, due to carelessness in their spiritual walk, while Jesus was away or because they had neglected to devote themselves to a time of prayer and fasting, they were unable to heal the boy.

Not only was Jesus dealing with the disciples' lack of faith, but the struggling faith of the child's father. "If You can do anything, have compassion on us and help us." Boldly, the father begs Jesus to "Help my unbelief!" How often are we caught in the struggle of our faith walk? We know the truths we read in Scripture with our head, but our heart falters with unbelief and skepticism, or we've become cynical. What do you do in those moments? Do you continue to walk in disbelief or self-sufficiency, questioning the goodness of God for your life? Or do you, like this father, cry in desperation to your Good Father, "Lord, help me in my unbelief?"

As Christ-followers, our faith must be cultivated, much like a field, the ground dug up and turned over repeatedly to ready the soil of our hearts to plant that tiny mustard seed of faith. God waters and nourishes our faith through our spiritual discipline and dedication to Him just as He cultivates the soil of our hearts, plants the seed, and nurtures it. Be encouraged, Dear One. God already knows your heart and struggles and is waiting for you to cry out to Him. Trust Him to strengthen your faith. Through this simple yet potent prayer, God stands ready to respond in compassion and love. AJW

date

scripture

PRAISE & THANKS

PRAYERS FOR MY

CHURCH

FAMILY&FRIENDS

NATION&WORLD

ON MY HEART TODAY

Day 9

The Power of a Pardon

Numbers 14:1-19

"And now, please let the power of the Lord be great as
you have promised...." (Numbers 14:17, ESV).

Grumbling and complaining... I love watching children who complain that there is nothing to do. From their limited perspective, life is simply not giving them what they want, and they are not happy. The reason I say that I love watching them is not that it brings me joy. Instead, it points right back to me and calls me guilty of the very same thing. I, too, quickly complain and find excuses to be miserable. The Old Testament shows human nature in proper form; we are up and down, over and over again. In today's Bible story, the people of Israel are once again unhappy and are making it known to Moses. God also noticed!

What is the problem? Remember that God delivered the people out of Egypt and promised to bring them to a new homeland. They were getting close to this land of promise. Moses recruited a team to go and see what the new land held in store for them and what would need to be done to move in. The problem? Giants lived in the land. Two men said it was not a problem for God. He would overcome and bring them safely to their new home. The other ten reported that they would not be able to defeat the giants. Human nature took over, and with no faith, all the people got scared and gave up before they even tried.

How often do we find ourselves overwhelmed by our circumstances, or even worse, we are afraid of and defeated by what we fear might happen? Learning to call upon God in prayers of faith is powerful praying. Moses, Aaron, Joshua, and Caleb knew, "the LORD is with us; do not fear them" (Numbers 14:9, ESV). So, silencing our fears results from remembering God is with us.

There is an interesting twist in this prayer of Moses. God tells Moses that He will destroy the people and make Moses great in a new and different way. It was a test of Moses' character and his leadership. Remember, "The Lord is not slow to fulfill his promise as some count slowness but is patient toward you, not wishing that any should perish, but that all should reach repentance" (2 Peter 3:9, ESV). Yes, God would have been justified in doing this, but He is gracious and loving. Moses could have taken the offer, but it would have been a selfish move and a failure of leadership.

This is the beauty of his prayer. Moses remembers that God made a promise to the people of Israel and He needs to show the non-Jewish world how great and good He is. Had Moses accepted the offer, God's reputation would have been questioned. So, Moses rejected the offer and passed the test. His prayer request was to let the power of the Lord be great, and pardon the iniquity of these people, according to the greatness of your steadfast love.

I do not know about you, but I dislike grumblers and complainers. I do not even like myself when I catch myself grumbling and complaining. Because I do not like it, I can be very impatient and unkind to people. I want to learn, like Moses, to resist the temptation to hurt people and give up on them when the noise comes. This is the heart of God, and it is powerful praying when I ask the Lord God to move me into his realm of gracious love and respond with kindness and gentleness. That request to let the power of the Lord be great in me and the situation is powerful. MPD

date

scripture

PRAISE & THANKS

PRAYERS FOR MY

CHURCH

FAMILY&FRIENDS

NATION&WORLD

ON MY HEART TODAY

Day 10

God, Have Mercy on Me

Psalm 51:1-19

"For I know my transgressions, and my sin is
ever before me" (Psalm 51:3, ESV).

"I was wrong." Those three words are so difficult to say. My wife and I will sometimes remember details differently and end up in a disagreement. I remember conversing about how long we had been attending a church. I thought it had only been a year, and she said it was more like two years. I felt she had to be wrong. It was an embarrassing argument because we were trying to make a good impression. The humor of it all is later, we reviewed the timeline and realized that the answer was 18 months! We were both wrong and off by six months.

Eventually, I can overcome my need to be correct and admit I was wrong, especially when the evidence is clear that I was off on my facts. Protecting my ego is not worth it if I harm my relationship with my wife or someone important to me. Sometimes, however, our sinful choices become something we try to hide or deny, especially if we are ashamed of our choices and behaviors or do not want to give up what we have chosen to do. When shame or wrong desires rule our world, we will likely fail to rise to the challenge of saying those three words: I was wrong.

One of the most infamous sins in the Bible is David's adulterous relationship with Bathsheba. He got intimately involved with another man's wife and then arranged to kill him to hide the transgression. The involvement with Bathsheba was terrible enough, but when he contemplated murder in his heart, it caused a ripple effect in David's heart. King David went about his life trying to avoid admitting that he was wrong. But God wants repentance. He requires us to own our wrongs and confess them. So God sent Nathan, the prophet, to help King David realize that he was wrong and that it was time to acknowledge his sin.

Sometimes we find ourselves being hardhearted and refusing to own our junk. Fortunately, King David realized his need to confess his sinful choices. He came to God and bared his soul. He acknowledged his sin before God. Psalm 51 reminds us that we must be ready and willing to confess our sins to God. Confession means we agree with God that our choices are wrong and admit this to God. Prayer allows us to own our wrongs and confess them to our Lord God. Prayer becomes a powerful tool for freedom and comfort when we are released from the guilt and shame of our sin through confession. Some may rebel against the idea of faith in God because it creates an unnecessary sense of guilt and shame. But I would argue that guilt and shame are natural to each of us, and faith in God is the remedy rather than the cause.

King David understood his guilt and shame and finally admitted his wrong actions to God. "For I know my transgressions, and my sin is ever before me. Against you, you only, have I sinned and done what is evil in your sight, so that you may be justified in your words and blameless in your judgment" (vs. 3-4, ESV). In his prayer of confession, King David found the remedy. "Purge me with hyssop, and I shall be clean; wash me, and I shall be whiter than snow. Let me hear joy and gladness; let the bones that you have broken rejoice" (vs. 7-8, ESV).

Life lessons can be learned as we get comfortable with confession and move to a willingness to admit our wrong actions, thoughts, and behaviors. Our sin is against God. Yes, we wrong others, and we need to be ready as often as necessary and as soon as possible to say to them, "I was wrong." Yet, the ultimate level of our problem is with God alone. It is His standards and guidance that we fail to follow, and it is both proper and necessary to say to God, "I was wrong."

Prayers of confession recognize our sinful hearts. We sin because we are sinful and rebellious people. Our prayers also acknowledge that we need God to cleanse and change us into righteous people. The Apostle John calls us to confession: "If we confess our sins, he is faithful and just to forgive us our sins and to cleanse us from all unrighteousness" (1 John 1:9, ESV).

King David serves as a model for our prayers of confession by asking God to restore our hearts to pursue what is right, restore our relationship with him, and restore our joy. Sin destroys us., It destroys our relationship with God, and it takes away our joy. When we admit our wrongs to God, it allows him to reclaim and restore us. Following confession, King David asks to be a teacher and an example to others. One of the most powerful lessons we can learn is to admit quickly and readily "I was wrong" to ourselves, others, and, most importantly, God. We will not be perfect in this life, but we can perfect our opportunities to show the grace and goodness of our God. He is ready and willing to forgive. He welcomes us to pray to Him to say, "I was wrong." MPD

date

scripture

PRAISE & THANKS

PRAYERS FOR MY

CHURCH

FAMILY&FRIENDS

NATION&WORLD

ON MY HEART TODAY

Day 11

Let This Cup Pass from Me

Matthew 26:36-46

"If it is possible, let this cup pass from Me. Yet not as
I will, but as You will." Matthew 26:39 HCSB

Have you ever endured a time of great despair that caused you to fall on your knees in anguished prayer? I have. It was a life or death situation that wasn't just my life in peril but the life of our unborn baby. For 72 hours, our lives hung in the balance. In grief and sorrow, my husband and I prayed fervently and continuously. God brought about a miraculous intervention; our oldest daughter was born and restored my health. However, we've also experienced the opposite result, and death entered our lives. In both situations, my husband and I prayed but acknowledged that we wanted God's will, whatever the outcome.

Jesus entered the Garden of Gethsemane, the place of an olive grove, with eleven of His disciples, commanding eight of them to stay at the entrance. Then, taking Peter, James, and John, He went further into the garden; His grief overwhelmed Him. Sharing His burden of anguish with them, Jesus asked them to remain with Him and keep vigil for Him. Then, going a little further into the garden, Jesus fell on His face and prayed to His Heavenly Father that if there was any other way to atone for man's sins, then to allow this cup to pass from Him if that was His Father's will.

This cup would mean imminent death and separation from His Father for the first time.

During His hour of greatest need, Jesus returned to His companions and found them sleeping. His prayer warriors fell asleep during His extreme wrestling with God's plan of salvation for all humanity. Grieved to the point of challenging Peter's firm declaration in the previous verses that even if others ran away or if he had to die with Jesus, Peter would never abandon Him. Again Jesus went away to pray. Alone. He was repeating His request to allow the cup of wrath as the propitiation, payment in full for man. A second time, He returned to find them sleeping. The three disciples' resting and sleeping were in stark contrast to Jesus' agonizing and exhausting prayer time.

I find it significant that Jesus went away to pray a third time, yet knowing He was the only way. He was the final sacrifice to reconcile sinful man to a Holy God. Jesus turned back to His three disciples and roused them awake. He knew His betrayer was on His way to sell Him into the hands of those who would demand His death. However, Jesus willingly gave up His life for the redemption of all humanity. Through His courageous confrontation to "drink of the cup," He fulfilled the Father's will (John 6:38), knowing that He could accomplish God's will through His death, burial, and resurrection. It was the only way to redeem humanity. Jesus, and only Jesus, could and would be made sin and a curse for all the world through His sacrificial death (2 Cor. 5:21; Gal. 3:13).

As Jesus entered the place of "an olive press," He, too, was pressed down with the enormity of what was about to transpire, sweating "great drops of blood" in His anguish (Luke 22:44). Jesus felt the awful burden of sin; His holy soul repelled by it. There was only one way, God's way, for us to have complete redemption. That way was the humble, obedient Son of God who lavishly displayed His love for us to offer the forgiveness of our trespasses and sins (Eph. 1:7).

Only one was perfect enough to carry the heavy cup of redemption. Christ took the cup of wrath to the cross. Jesus endured the cross and crushed death's blow, offering forgiveness and reconciliation to His Heavenly Father through Him alone. So pray with me, thanking God for His incredible gift of redemption made possible through His Son.

Prayer--Heavenly Father, Thank you for the gift of Jesus' sacrifice to offer as payment in my place for all the bad things I have ever done and ever will do. I can't imagine the excruciating pain of being separated from your Holy Son for me. Strengthen me to watch and pray, even when it's hard. Amen AJW

date

scripture

PRAISE & THANKS

PRAYERS FOR MY

CHURCH

FAMILY&FRIENDS

NATION&WORLD

ON MY HEART TODAY

Day 12

Not My Will but Yours

Luke 22:39-46

"Father, if You are willing, take this cup away from Me—
nevertheless, not My will, but Yours, be done."
Luke 22:42 HSCB

"I don't want that cup!" screamed the child. "I want the cup you gave him!" Then, in a full-blown temper tantrum, the child commanded the attention of all observing the spectacle. The mother, wholly embarrassed and frustrated, took the coveted cup from her son and gave it to her demanding daughter. Then, turning around, the mother gave the unwanted cup to the son, who stood quietly watching the drama. How often in life are we given something we don't want? What has been your response? Sadly, I probably have had a few temper tantrums that only God has known, and maybe a few that my family has had front-row seats to watch. However, one person accepted a cup that was decidedly the most difficult. Jesus.

Jesus' earthly ministry was quickly coming to an end; His death loomed darkly before Him. Entering the Garden of Gethsemane with eleven of His dearest friends, Jesus withdrew a little from them and began praying earnestly. "Father, if You are willing, take this cup away from Me–nevertheless, not My will but Yours be done." Praying so intensely that sweat-like drops of blood fell from His body. The agony of what He was about to experience pressed down on Him, squeezing from Him the blood that would save the world.

Meeting His Father there in the "garden of the olive press" to seek strength as Jesus faced great suffering. If there was another way to offer forgiveness for the sins of humanity, Jesus prayed, please let this current path of redemption pass from me, but if not, let it be done. Ironically, human history began in a garden (Gen. 2:7-25), and the Redeemed Children's story will end in a "garden city" (Rev. 21:1-27). In the middle is the Garden of Gethsemane, where Jesus accepted the cup of sorrow, pain, suffering, and ultimately death from the Father's hand.

Knowing His soul would experience the most profound agony in what was to come, knowing the humiliation, abuse, and suffering shame that He would bear on the cross, Jesus willingly allowed the will of the Father to have the preeminence. Jesus would be made sin for the world, taking that pain upon His body. However, the most profound agony He would endure would be the separation from His Father for the first and only time in eternity, past and future. God the Father would turn His back on His Son, who became the filthiness of humankind's sin. This solemn experience Jesus called "drinking the cup."

There was no other way to pay the penalty of sin. Simply Jesus was the only perfect sacrifice that could offer propitiation, the payment, for man. Laying aside His will, He obeyed His Father's will. Through humility, Christ endured on the cross, bearing the weight of the world, conquering the power of sin and death in His resurrection. In that, we can rejoice with the Apostle Paul wrote in 2 Corinthians 5:21, "He made the One who did not know sin to be sin for us so that we might become the righteousness of God in Him." It was the only way that we could be made righteous. Jesus must drink the cup His Father had for Him, and because of that, we can have eternal life with Him in Heaven for all eternity! AJW

date *scripture*

PRAISE
& THANKS

PRAYERS FOR MY

CHURCH

FAMILY&FRIENDS

NATION&WORLD

ON MY HEART TODAY

Day 13

The Forever Kingdom for King David

---

2 Samuel 7:1-29

"For you, O LORD of hosts, the God of Israel, have made this
revelation to your servant, saying, 'I will build you a house'"
(2 Samuel 7:27, ESV).

I needed to take my wife to an appointment a few days ago. She had
the address and placed it into the GPS on her phone. Directions started
flowing out, but I headed in a different direction. Even though the GPS
would have a faster and shorter route, I knew that traffic would be more
challenging if I went the way the GPS recommended. I also liked my
street options better. Eventually, my path and the recommended path
converged, and there was harmony. This is the experience of King David
that we find in today's Bible passage. We are introduced to his conversation
with the prophet Nathan in 2 Samuel 7 and, eventually, his prayer with
the Lord God.

King David was at rest from war and was interested in building a
temple for the Lord God to dwell among the people of Israel. If the king
has an admirable house, how much more should the Lord God? Nathan
tells David to proceed with his idea, but God has something different in
mind. God is not ready for this king to build a temple. The task of building
the temple would be saved for King David's son. With God's new and
unmistakable message, Nathan returns to King David to tell him that

he should not build the temple. However, the Lord God has something greater for King David. The Lord God gives a covenant promise to the King. This promise is referred to as the Davidic Covenant. It is a promise that God will provide King David an heir on the throne of Israel forever. "When your days are fulfilled, and you lie down with your fathers, I will raise your offspring after you, who shall come from your body, and I will establish his kingdom. He shall build a house for my name, and I will establish the throne of his kingdom forever" (2 Samuel 7:12-13, ESV). The promise begins with King Solomon, but God brings ultimate fulfillment in our Lord Jesus Christ. To his mother, Mary, God promised her son would be the forever heir to the Davidic throne. "And the angel said to her, 'Do not be afraid, Mary, for you have found favor with God. And behold, you will conceive in your womb and bear a son, and you shall call his name Jesus. He will be great and will be called the Son of the Most High. And the Lord God will give to him the throne of his father David, and he will reign over the house of Jacob forever, and of his kingdom, there will be no end" (Luke 1:30-33, ESV).

The Lord God is a covenant-giving, promise-keeping God. He promised Abraham a great heritage and that he would bless all nations. God promises King David an eternal throne fulfilled by the Messiah, Jesus. God's nature is to generously bless with His promises and then commit to ultimately fulfilling those promises. So how does that help us to pray with power? We pray to claim the promises of God and to live according to these promises. Then we ask the Spirit of God to guide us and help us understand how God's promises will guide our lives.

I would like to know if you are like me. When I decide on a plan and begin to follow it, I do not like to be deterred. But life often has its interruptions, and it is frustrating. Sometimes the brokenness of our world causes these interruptions, but remember, the realm of our planet is still under the sovereign care of our Lord God. Sometimes, as in God redirecting King David, God Himself will interrupt and turn us. Our prayers will help us to ask, discuss, and even complain to God. "God, I don't understand!" But then, our prayers must claim what God has promised to us. "And we know that for those who love God all things work together for good, for those who are called according to his purpose" (Romans 8:28, ESV).

The Lord, our God, knows what is best for us, and He knows what will accomplish His purposes and bring Him glory. Looking back to King David, he humbly and wisely accepts the promises and leading of the Lord God. He sits before the throne of God and gladly accepts what God has planned for him. This is powerful praying! When we stop long enough to hear and understand how God's promises work in our lives, we can humbly and gratefully accept what He has in store for us. There have been many times when what I thought would work out best did not, and I can see that God had something better for me. What about the situations where we pray and do not see how God is leading? We pray in faith the promise that God is good, and He will accomplish His good in our lives. This is powerful praying! MPD

date

scripture

PRAISE & THANKS

PRAYERS FOR MY

CHURCH

FAMILY&FRIENDS

NATION&WORLD

ON MY **HEART TODAY**

Day 14

There is None Like You

---

1 Chronicles 17:16-27

"There is none like you, O LORD, and there is no
God besides you, according to all that we have heard
with our ears" (1 Chronicles 17:20, ESV).

I remember hearing the term "Big Godder" and it came to my mind as I read today's passage. So, I went to the internet to see if I could find the origin of the term. Robert Dick Wilson was a professor of Hebrew at Princeton Theological Seminary, and from my research, it looks like he is the originator of the term. After listening to Dr. Donald Grey Barnhouse, a former student who returned to preach at Princeton, the Professor told Dr. Barnhouse that he was glad to see he was a "Big Godder." Dr. Barnhouse asked for an explanation. Professor Wilson responded that some preachers have a little God who does not do miracles and care for his people. But for others, they speak of a great God. "He speaks, it is done. He commands, and it stands fast. He knows how to show himself strong on behalf of them that fear him." (https://edtaylor.org/2020/01/10/are-you-a-big-godder/).

A worthy question is whether we are a "Big Godder" or a "Little Godder"? When we pray, do we believe that God is more significant than our problems and can do all He promises to do? Our prayers will carry victory because we believe that our God is the Almighty God. We believe He is all-wise, so He knows what is best for us. God delights in surprising us with better paths and a greater preferred future if we will ask and then trust Him to care for us. King David was surprised by this big and mighty God! As King, he wanted to build a house for God so the people of Israel would have a place to worship God.

It was a noble desire, and God would allow for this Temple to be built by King David's son, Solomon. For now, God wanted to take over and do something greater for David and to promise something that would have eternal value. God promised King David that He would establish his throne forever. "Moreover, I declare to you that the LORD will build you a house. When your days are fulfilled to walk with your fathers, I will raise up your offspring after you, one of your own sons, and I will establish his kingdom. He shall build a house for me, and I will establish his throne forever" (1 Chronicles 17:10-12, ESV).

The promises of the Lord God are credible because He is a big God. As we learned in 2 Samuel 7 and now in 1 Chronicles 17, this Davidic Covenant is God's gracious promise to King David to bless him. In response to this covenant promise, King David sits before God and realizes his smallness in comparison to the greatness of God. His expression to God is a realization of a big God doing big things for him. "There is none like you, O LORD, and there is no God besides you, according to all that we have heard with our ears" (1 Chronicles 17:20, ESV).

We pray to a big God. He is sovereign, all-powerful, all-knowing, and present everywhere. Because God is so great, He can always do what He promises and do better and greater things than we can imagine. The Apostle Paul reminds us of God's more excellent vision and capacity. "Now to him who is able to do far more abundantly than all that we ask or think, according to the power at work within us, to him be glory in the church and in Christ Jesus throughout all generations, forever and ever. Amen" (Ephesians 3:20-21, ESV). Our prayers become powerful when we place our trust in the capable hands and all-accomplishing power of God, this God who can do "far more"!

There is still more to learn from King David in powerful praying prayers. King David accepted the Lord God's preferred path and welcomed the opportunity to bring glory to God. As our Lord Jesus Christ taught the disciples, we seek for the will of God to be done on earth like it is in heaven because it displays God's kingdom, power, and glory. Therefore, praying and asking for God to be glorified in our lives is critical to understanding our place under the protective banner of God. Our life goal should be to bring glory to God. As the Westminster Confession reminds us, our chief goal in life is the glory of God.

One additional prayer tip we learn from King David. He accepts the Lord God's better path for him with gratitude. His prayer almost displays a sense of giddiness! Sovereign Lord, You would do this for me? I do not deserve it, but I am very grateful. Our prayer journey is a journey of learning to submit our will and desires to the superior will and desires of the Lord God. And then, even beyond that step, to accept it with gratitude and celebration. "Now you have been pleased to bless the house of your servant, that it may continue forever before you, for it is you, O LORD, who have blessed, and it is blessed forever" (1 Chronicles 17:27, ESV). Lord God, your promises are amazing, and I accept! That is powerful praying! MPD

date

scripture

PRAISE
& THANKS

PRAYERS FOR MY

CHURCH

FAMILY&FRIENDS

NATION&WORLD

ON MY HEART TODAY

Day 15

David Blessed the Lord

1 Chronicles 29:10-19

"And now we thank you, our God, and praise your
glorious name" (1 Chronicles 29:13, ESV).

A few years ago, a psychologist friend reminded me how important it is
to develop gratitude. Specifically, he encouraged me to look back over the
day at the end of each day and list three "thanksgivings" for that day. This
prayer of King David in today's Bible passage is most definitely a prayer
of gratitude and thanksgiving. The King is amazed at the generosity of
God and the people as they prepare for the future King Solomon to build
the Temple. Remember that King David wanted to build the Temple, but
God withheld that role from him and assured him that his son would be
given the responsibility. King David accepted the will of God and decided
(with God's blessing) that he would gather the resources needed to build
the Temple. With a generous gift from King David and donations from
the people now in place, King David gives thanks to God for guiding the
people to this place of abundance and preparation.

The King offers a beautiful opening of worship in this public prayer.
Do not miss the majesty of God in his description. "Therefore David
blessed the LORD in the presence of all the assembly. And David said:
"Blessed are you, O LORD, the God of Israel our father, forever and
ever. Yours, O LORD, is the greatness and the power and the glory and

the victory and the majesty, for all that is in the heavens and in the earth is yours. Yours is the kingdom, O LORD, and you are exalted as head above all" (1 Chronicles 29:10-11, ESV). His prayer follows his counsel to "Ascribe to the Lord the glory due his name; worship the Lord in the splendor of holiness" (Psalm 29:2, ESV).

Additionally, King David acknowledges that God owns everything. God gives all that we have, and he must be recognized as the rightful owner. "Both riches and honor come from you, and you rule over all. In your hand are power and might, and in your hand, it is to make great and to give strength to all" (1 Chronicles 29:12, ESV). Our prayers allow us to remind ourselves and let our Lord God know that we receive everything from Him, and that He is the abundant giver. Through our prayers, we offer our gratitude for His wonderful gifts.

King David reminds the people in this prayer that the abundance they offered for the Temple was made possible by the generous care of the Lord God. God is good and gives to us abundantly. He delights in us also adopting an abundant and generous mindset. The King acknowledged that the people were "offering freely and joyously to you" (I Chronicles 29:17, ESV).

Some people naturally have a generous spirit. But rather than taking pride in that, our prayers shift the glory to God. We recognize the work of God in our hearts and the provisions He gives. Not only do we learn principles of giving for our Christian journey, but we also learn to enrich our prayers as we give thanks to God for His grace at work in our lives.

"And God is able to make all grace abound to you so that having all sufficiency in all things at all times, you may abound in every good work. As it is written, "He has distributed freely, he has given to the poor; his righteousness endures forever." He who supplies seed to the sower and bread for food will supply and multiply your seed for sowing and increase the harvest of your righteousness. You will be enriched in every way to be generous in every way, which through us will produce thanksgiving to God" (2 Corinthians 9:8-11, ESV).

For those of us who have a little more trouble letting go of our wealth and treasures, our prayers can be a journey of asking God to help us trust Him to provide through His abundant grace and make us more generous and less selfish. This empowers us to learn and experience the joys of generosity and grow our trust in God. More confidence in God and less faith in our wealth and earthly treasures.

King David concludes his prayer with a request that his son will be faithful and obedient to the Lord God and then successful in completing the Temple. From his son, King Solomon, we also see this wise counsel to "Commit your work to the LORD, and your plans will be established." (Proverbs 16:3, ESV). With our gifts and thanksgiving, we can ask the Lord God to bless what we offer to accomplish His purposes and to bring the work to completion. Trusting God to give and work through the gifts for the preferred results is powerful praying! MPD

date

scripture

PRAISE
& THANKS

PRAYERS FOR MY

CHURCH

FAMILY&FRIENDS

NATION&WORLD

ON MY HEART TODAY

Day 16

Hope, Inheritance, and Power

Ephesians 1:15-19

"I pray that the God of our Lord Jesus Christ, the glorious Father,
would give you a spirit of wisdom and revelation in the knowledge
of Him. I pray that the perception of your mind may be enlightened
so you may know what is the hope of His calling, what are the
glorious riches of His inheritance among the saints, and what is the
immeasurable greatness of His power to us who believe, according
to the working of His vast strength." Ephesians 1:17-19 HSCB

"She had gone down in history as "America's Greatest Miser," yet when
she died in 1916, "Hetty" Green left an estate valued at over $100 million.
She ate cold oatmeal because it cost to heat it. Her son had to suffer a leg
amputation because she delayed so long in looking for a free clinic that
his case became incurable. She was wealthy, yet she chose to live like a
pauper."3 What a powerful illustration of how we often live as believers,
with limitless wealth from God our Father, living like beggars in the street.

Paul's genuine love and concern for the believers at Ephesus was
evident in his prayer for them to possess divine insight into the wealth of
spiritual resources through Jesus Christ. In these verses, Paul prayed for
the church's spiritual perception, exhibiting true Christian character. As
we grow in the knowledge of God, the Holy Spirit reveals truth through
the Word of God, which gives us the wisdom to understand and apply it

to our lives. Through the power of the Holy Spirit, we can practice daily, renewing our minds through God's transforming power (Romans 12:2).

Before we come to a saving knowledge of the grace of Christ, we are beggars. Living life in sin, alienated from a God who loves us, wallowing in our poverty of spirit (Isaiah 64). When we know God personally through His Son, we are set apart in Him, declared holy and just. We have been "called out" of our sin by grace into a holy calling (2 Timothy 1:9), out of darkness into marvelous light (1 Peter 2:9). It is in this beautiful grace that we have hope for our future in Christ. The "hope of our calling" should encourage us as we daily walk in the Spirit to be pure, obedient, and faithful to the gospel message of Christ.

We also share in His great inheritance; at the same time, the church is part of the greatest treasure of that inheritance! The Father receives glory from the church because of His investment of Jesus Christ into our lives. Knowing such a great price was paid on our behalf should encourage us to a life of devotion and dedication to the Lord. Christ paid a steep price for each one of us. The church is His inheritance, but we are privileged to share Christ's inheritance. Eternity with Him in His Heaven.

Paul continues to pray that believers understand the "exceeding greatness of [God's] power." with truth so tremendous that he used several Greek words to clarify his point. Because of the powerful working of a mighty God who gives power to His children, we have been given His divine dynamic with boundless energy as we continue to live our lives worthy of His calling. Just like "Hetty" Green, what good is it for us to have this wealth at our disposal if we are too weak or unwilling to use it?

We share in the resurrection of Jesus Christ through God's immeasurable power. Because of that we become the glory of the Son as we present ourselves as a living sacrifice, holy and acceptable to God (Romans 12:1). Our "living hope" will be realized as God's immeasurable greatness brings us safely to the abundant riches of Heaven's "final glory". AJW

3 The Bible Exposition Commentary Vol. 2, Wiersbe, p. 8

date

scripture

PRAISE & THANKS

PRAYERS FOR MY

CHURCH

FAMILY&FRIENDS

NATION&WORLD

ON MY HEART TODAY

Day 17

Know the Love of Christ

Ephesians 3:14-21

"I pray that He may grant you, according to the riches of His glory, to be strengthened with power in the inner man through His Spirit and that the Messiah may dwell in your hearts through faith. I pray that you, being rooted and firmly established in love, may be able to comprehend with all the saints what is the length and width, height and depth of God's love, and to know the Messiah's love that surpasses knowledge so that you may be filled with all the fullness of God." Ephesians 3:16-19 HCSB

Iowa has experienced a new phenomenon called "Derecho," described as an "inland hurricane," a widespread, long-lasting, fast-moving thunderstorm with straight winds. If you live in Iowa, you have either lived through, had damage, or know someone that has suffered damage from these mighty storms. One of many tragedies that result from a derecho is the destruction of trees. I recently read an article advising people who are still re-planting trees from the last derecho in 2021.

The article stated that when you transplant trees, you are not to water them daily. The report indicated that you are to water only every few days. The purpose behind this? So that trees do not become dependent upon outside factors for their water, teaching the tree's roots to dig deep into the soil. When the roots go deep, the tree is nourished and stabilized. If the tree is watered by outside sources such as a hose or a bucket, it teaches the roots to live at a shallow level. So that if another fierce storm happens, the tree will easily topple and die.

Looking at Paul's letter to the Ephesians, he addresses several matters. Central to his letter is his prayer of a beautiful, poignant request for the believers' spiritual power. Paul's prayer asks God for three things; that believers be equipped with inner strength, insightful understanding, and spiritual excellence. Why would he pray these things for the believers?

Like the believers in Paul's day, trials and challenges threaten our faith today. The prayer begins with a request from God to bless believers with inner power. Through that power, the indwelling of Christ is in the hearts of each believer. Through the power of the Trinity, we are strengthened by God, rooted deeply and Jesus as He dwells in us, and filled with all the fullness of God through the Holy Spirit.

It's not just enough to know what God has done for us through the power of the Holy Spirit in the person of Jesus Christ, and we need to know how to put these tools to use. If our roots in God are shallow, we will be like the man who built his house on the sand. When the storms come, our faith will falter (Matthew 7:24-26). However, as we lay ahold of God's riches of understanding, being rooted in Scripture, and spend time daily with God and prayer, we can weather the storms of life (Psalm 1:3).

The progression of Paul's prayer is four-fold. First, he prays that the inner man might have spiritual strength. Through spiritual power, we can experience Christ on a deeper level, enabling us to "get ahold" or apprehend God's great love for us through His Son Jesus Christ. We then are filled with the fullness of God through the Holy Spirit. Through the Trinity, our lives are nourished and stabilized, with deep roots in His immeasurable wealth: the height, depth, width, and length. The foundation of our faith is built then on the stability of Christ, in Whom is the vastness of God's power found. As trees planted by streams of water, our goal should be to experience God's effectual power at work in our lives, motivated by our desire to bring glory to God. AJW

date

scripture

PRAISE & THANKS

PRAYERS FOR MY

CHURCH

FAMILY&FRIENDS

NATION&WORLD

ON MY HEART TODAY

Day 18

Save Us, Please!

---

2 Kings 19:14-19

"So now, O LORD our God, save us, please, from his
hand, that all the kingdoms of the earth may know that
you, O LORD, are God alone" (2 Kings 19:19, ESV).

King George VI's prayer on D-Day called the people of the British Commonwealth to pray. He acknowledged the overwhelming challenge before them and the need for God to intervene. "At this historic moment, surely not one of us is too busy, too young, or too old to play a part in a nationwide, perchance worldwide, the vigil of prayer as the great crusade sets forth. If from every place of worship, from home and factory, from men and women of all ages and many races and occupations, our intercessions rise, then, please God, both now and in the future, not remote, the predictions of an ancient Psalm may be fulfilled: "The Lord will give strength unto his people: the Lord will give his people the blessing of peace" (https://www.royal.uk/king-georgevis- speech-dday).

Whether as a nation or as an individual, we have heard the stories and even experienced those times when the situation is dire, and the need to pray becomes essential. The same applied to King Hezekiah as he faced King Sennacherib, who had a far superior army than Judah's. In today's Bible passage, King Hezekiah turns to the Temple and calls upon the Lord God to deliver the nation. Prayer becomes our opportunity to turn to the

Lord, express our trust in Him, and ask Him to deliver and save us. As we pray to the Lord, our hearts are calmed, and we can lay out our desire for God to intervene and accomplish His will.

King Hezekiah's prayer shows his resolve to put his trust in God. His prayer begins with an acknowledgment of the mighty standing of God. He sees that God is the One "enthroned above the Cherubim." He is the Covenant-keeping God of Israel. He is the God of all kingdoms. "You are the God, you alone, of all the kingdoms of the earth" (2 Kings 19:15, ESV). There is only one God, and He is sovereign and reigns over all governments.

Furthermore, He is the creator of all governments. If He is powerful enough to create the world, He is then powerful enough to deliver His people from the Assyrian army. King Hezekiah's trust is in this all-powerful God. Our prayers become powerful as we embrace the omnipotent God and express our trust in Him.

King Hezekiah acknowledged the truth of Sennacherib when he claimed victory over other nations. Sennacherib taunts the God of Judah in this claim, but King Hezekiah knows the difference is the gods of these other nations are wood and stone. Our prayers are powerful because we pray to the True and Living God. The Apostle Paul reminded the Thessalonians they had been introduced to this True and Living God. "For not only has the word of the Lord sounded forth from you in Macedonia and Achaia, but your faith in God has gone forth everywhere so that we need not say anything. For they themselves report concerning us the kind of reception we had among you, and how you turned to God from idols to serve the living and true God" (1 Thessalonians 1:8-9, ESV). Our prayers to God are more than just a mental exercise to calm ourselves or focus our thoughts. Instead, our hearts reach the God of Heaven and claim the privilege of calling upon Him to help us in our time of need.

The bottom line for King Hezekiah is to ask God to deliver Judah. "So now, O LORD our God, save us, please, from his hand, that all the kingdoms of the earth may know that You, O LORD, are God alone" (2 Kings 19:19, ESV). Right to the point, "Save us!" King Hezekiah's prayer is a testament to the world that you, "O Lord, are God alone." Our prayers take on maturity and power as we learn to submit our requests to the ultimate purpose of God and His glory. God delights in caring for us and answering our prayers. We delight in bringing glory to Him as He alone deserves. This is powerful praying! MPD

date

scripture

PRAISE & THANKS

PRAYERS FOR MY

CHURCH

FAMILY&FRIENDS

NATION&WORLD

ON MY HEART TODAY

Day 19

A Gift of Added Life

Isaiah 38:1-8

"Please, O LORD, remember how I have walked before
you in faithfulness and with a whole heart, and have done
what is good in your sight" (Isaiah 38:3, ESV).

You owe me! Generally, I enjoy doing nice things for others. After all, we are challenged by the Bible to look out for the interests of others. But there are times when someone needs help, and I resent being asked. So, I take care of the need, and then I either think or say, you owe me! I can say it in a lighthearted way, but my words and thoughts have an edge, and they betray the gracious spirit I should live out. My heart should be willing to do for others without expecting a reward or, even worse, hold the favor over the other person, so they feel like they are indebted to me.

We can get into this dangerous game with God. When this was brought to my attention a few years ago, I wrestled with it. Indeed, I do not have this attitude toward God. But I had to admit that I did. It goes something like this. God, I am living a good Christian life, so You have to get me out of this mess. Or, I am a pastor, so You owe it to me to provide for me since I have dedicated my life to ministry. Let me clarify, God promises and delight in taking care of us and providing for our needs, especially when we follow our Lord Jesus Christ's command to seek His Kingdom first. But, when we show a demanding attitude and a sort of spoiled brat mindset that God somehow owes us, we are in trouble. I want to be cautious, but it almost seems in today's Bible passage that King Hezekiah is telling God that He owes him. God must let King Hezekiah live because of all the good that this King has done for God.

This prayer of Hezekiah may be one of the most challenging prayers to study in our 40-day journey. It initially appears that Hezekiah is telling God that the news of his impending death is not what he deserves. Then Hezekiah turned his face to the wall, prayed to the LORD, and said, "Please, O LORD, remember how I have walked before you in faithfulness and with a whole heart and have done what is good in your sight." (Isaiah 38:2-3, ESV).

While admitting my perception of King Hezekiah's prayer, the story's intrigue is that God responds favorably with an additional fifteen years of life for Hezekiah. So, perhaps there is something underneath this prayer that is different from my initial conclusions. First, we need to know that Hezekiah's father was an ungodly king, and his son also chose not to follow after the Lord God. Hezekiah was the exception of a godly king in a line of ungodly kings. He was a man of prayer, and he was a man who chose to follow after the God of King David. This story of King Hezekiah is found in 2 Kings 20 and 2 Chronicles 34. I decided on this Isaiah passage because of the added writing of King Hezekiah describing his journey from facing death to being gifted additional years of life. His writing helps us to see the faith his prayer demonstrated to the Lord God. "Behold, it was for my welfare that I had great bitterness; but in love, you have delivered my life from the pit of destruction, for you have cast all my sin behind your back" (Isaiah 38:17, ESV).

King Hezekiah's prayer allows us to talk about ways that we should not pray, as well as ways that we should pray. Our prayers are not occasions for us to list our accomplishments in a way that we try to impress God. We know that our relationship with God is based on faith in Him, not trust in our works and efforts. Our prayers are not to be used for our selfish desires. Prayer is our opportunity to bring our selfish impulses in line with God's preferred and good purposes. We can wrestle with God in humility, but our prayers must not ever be a rant that demands God should do it our way or give us what we want. So, why do I think King Hezekiah's prayer was not selfish?

As mentioned, Hezekiah was a King who sought after God. "He trusted in the LORD, the God of Israel, so there was none like him among all the kings of Judah after him, nor among those who were before him. For he held fast to the LORD. He did not depart from following him but kept the commandments that the LORD commanded Moses" (2 Kings 18:5-6, ESV). His prayer about what he had done reminded the Lord God that he trusted in the God of King David, unlike some of the other Kings of Judah. On the positive side of the principles of prayer, we can learn to tell God of our heart's desire to follow and obey Him. "Lord, I have trusted in Jesus Christ for my salvation, and I continue to trust in You today. Now, Lord, please be honored to answer my prayers because You have invited me to ask anything of you." This falls right in line with the instructions of our Lord Jesus, "Whatever you ask in my name, I will do, that the Father may be glorified in the Son. If you ask me anything in my name, I will do It" (John 14:13-14, ESV). Our prayers become powerful as we offer requests that align with the name of Jesus. They fit our Lord's purposes, are pleasing to our Lord, and fulfill our Lord's glory.

Another key for King Hezekiah is his awareness and commitment to the covenant promises to King David. King Hezekiah wanted to continue his reign in Judah, so he could participate in the promises of God to have King David's throne continue forever. I believe God answered King Hezekiah's prayer was because of his faith and fidelity to the Davidic Covenant and the God of that covenant. Our prayers depend on God responding to them to accomplish His ultimate purposes.

So, can we pray for God to do a miracle of healing and request that God will not allow someone to die? Of course! One of the problems with our prayers is that we do not experience God's power because we pray too small. No one can blame King Hezekiah for wanting to continue to live, which is true for us. Why would we not ask God to continue the life of our loved ones and friends or even our own life? Pray big! Pray boldly! No small prayers become our new challenge. But we must be willing to allow God to be the final determiner. We pray big prayers with the commitment of "nevertheless, not as I will, but as you will" (Matthew 26:39, ESV). Praying big and confidently and praying humbly while trusting the highest authority of our great God and His ultimate purposes. This is learning to access the power of the Lord Almighty, and it is powerful praying! MPD

date

scripture

PRAISE & THANKS

PRAYERS FOR MY

CHURCH

FAMILY&FRIENDS

NATION&WORLD

ON MY HEART TODAY

Day 20

Because of God's Great Mercy

Daniel 9:4-19

"Listen, my God, and hear. Open Your eyes and see our desolation. For we are not presenting our petitions before You based on our righteous acts, but based on Your abundant compassion." Daniel 9:18 HCSB

Our family motto is "Choices and Consequences." What had started as a lighthearted joke had a deeper meaning. As our children grew, they began to understand that their choices sometimes had lasting consequences, good and bad. For example, a friend shared with me a similar thought she had with her 16-year-old daughter. "I'm trying to get her to understand the choices she makes as a 16-year-old can have long-lasting, even lifetime consequences." The prophet Daniel, exiled to Babylon when he was 15, now 81 years old, comprehended that Israel's sinful choices had long-lasting consequences.

While Daniel studied the book of Jeremiah and its prophecy, God used the prophetic words to reveal to Daniel the consequences of Israel's rebelliousness. Jerusalem would suffer catastrophic destruction. Immediately, Daniel turned his attention to the Lord in prayer and petition, with fasting, sackcloth, and ashes, typical behavior of a penitent heart as he expressed deep sorrow and remorse. No matter how often we read scripture, God's inspired word is applicable and unchanging, revealing something to be learned even when we've repeatedly read the same passage (2 Tim. 3:16).

Daniel began with a call to worship the awe-inspiring God. We're often tempted to jump into a "to-do list" for God, but humbled, he prepared to make his heart right with God through fasting and prayer. After spending time worshiping, Daniel begins his confession of intercessory prayer. God doesn't need to wait for an entire nation to repent but will start working when a faithful intercessor begins to pray (James 5:16).

Daniel's prayer then moves to the Lord's faithfulness as the covenant-keeping God of Israel. The children of Israel had broken their covenant with God and had no right to call on His covenanted name. However, Daniel began to petition God for mercy and forgiveness, not only for himself but for the nation. When we pause to confess our iniquities and the iniquities of our country, God will remember us.

Daniel focused on God's compassion, mercy, and forgiveness, not only that Israel would be restored, glorifying God's Holy Name. He begged God to extend mercy, not giving them what they truly deserved. Israel had chosen sin, doing wrong, acting wickedly, rebelling, and turning away from their Covenant-Keeping God. The natural consequence was God's chastening hand on a rebellious nation (Deut. 29:25), but God is a compassionate God, full of grace and mercy. Daniel reminded God of His promise to them. "If my people who are called by my name will humble themselves, and pray and seek my face and turn from their wicked ways, then I will hear from heaven and will forgive their sin and heal their land." (2 Chron. 7:14)

The consequences will naturally follow when we refuse to repent and confess our sins. Daniel had lived almost 70 years in exile and knew God was about to restore Israel. May we be a people of repentance and confession, knowing that God will continue to glorify His name through His children. "Lord, hear! Lord, forgive! Lord, listen and act!"

No matter how often we read scripture, God's inspired word is applicable. There is always something to be learned even when we've read the same passage repeatedly (2 Tim. 3:16). AJW

date

scripture

PRAISE & THANKS

PRAYERS FOR MY

CHURCH

FAMILY&FRIENDS

NATION&WORLD

ON MY **HEART** TODAY

Day 21

Christ Dwelling in You

Philippians 1:9-11

"I pray this: that your love will keep on growing in knowledge and every kind of discernment so that you can approve the things that are superior and can be pure and blameless in the day of Christ, filled with the fruit of righteousness that comes through Jesus Christ to the glory and praise of God" Philippians 1:9-11 HSCB

I was in 3rd grade when I began to attend an after-school kids' club at a local church called JOY Club. JOY represented "Jesus, Others, and You". Children gathered from around town and a few of the closer small towns to enjoy an afternoon of cookies, punch, games, stories, and Bible study. I remember one older couple dedicated their time and talents to minister to the needs of rambunctious after-school children. Gwen and Jim didn't have any children, marrying later in life. Both had been missionaries to different countries, returning to central Iowa to retire.

Gwen and Jim were a picture of what Paul prayed for in the lives of the believers in Philippi. Their conduct was evident in a growing love for others, Christian character, and service. I would watch them interact with the boys and girls, especially me. But, growing up, I always wanted to be like them. They were Jesus' representatives here on earth, radiating joy in furthering the Gospel of Christ.

Paul's prayer for his dear friends in Philippi is two-fold. First, he prays for them to have a growing love for others and to develop Christian maturity in character and service. Love born out of selfless action and concern for others through knowledge and discernment is the maturity of the Christian life. Through agape love and abiding maturity in Christ, believers experience what matters here on earth. As we grow in Him, we will experience the fruit of righteousness Paul prays for in the believer's lives.

Spiritual fruit is produced in the life of a believer through continual growth and maturity in our walk with God. We will bear marks of the "fruit of the Spirit" with a character that glorifies God, bringing joy to others and ourselves (Gal. 5:22-23). The "fruit" spoken of here is in winning lost souls (Rom. 1:13), every good work we do on Christ's behalf (Col. 1:10), and through our praise and worship of God (Heb. 13:15). This "spiritual fruit" brings glory to Jesus beautifully and excellently. This fruit doesn't require accolades or recognition because Christ is our focus. A word of warning, however, "religious" fruit done in our strength simply falls flat, bringing glory to ourselves, dismissing the credit that should be God's glory alone.

Through our selfless love for others, Paul continues to pray that we would grow in our character and service to God. A person with a mature or sincere character doesn't live lives that cause others to stumble but has been tested and found worthy of exercising spiritual discernment and is without offense. Like Gwen and Jim, their mature character and faithful love filled their lives with spiritual fruit from Christ dwelling in their hearts and minds. When we allow Christ to dwell in us, He will produce spiritual fruit in our lives that bring glory to God. This kind of fellowship results in selfless love and mature character with service that brings others "JOY." AJW

In what ways are you producing spiritual fruit?

What can you do to bring joy to the world around you?

date

scripture

PRAISE & THANKS

PRAYERS FOR MY

CHURCH

FAMILY&FRIENDS

NATION&WORLD

ON MY HEART TODAY

Day 22

Walk Worthy of Christ

Colossians 1:9-14

"We are asking that you may be filled with the knowledge of His will in all wisdom and spiritual understanding so that you may walk worthy of the Lord, fully pleasing to Him, bearing fruit in every good work and growing in the knowledge of God. May you be strengthened with all power according to His glorious might for all endurance and patience, with joy giving thanks to the Father who has enabled you to share in the saints inheritance in the light." Colossians 1:9- 12 HCSB

There he stood—my 7th-grade science teacher. Shame and reproach caused me almost to turn around and run. As a 35-year-old woman, I remembered my naughty and sometimes disrespectful behavior in Mr. Kline's science classroom. "The me I am today is not the "me" that used to be," I told myself. Then, taking a deep breath, hand in hand with my two daughters, I approached the aging teacher. "I'm not sure if you remember me, Mr. Kline, but I want you to know that I grew up to be a godly wife and mother." His gentle eyes crinkled in recognition, and a broad smile crossed his face, "Why, of course, I remember you! I did not doubt that you would be a fine woman one day." So we stood there and chatted for several minutes as I shared with him how my life changed as I grew in the Lord over the years.

God taught me something powerful in those moments. He reminded me that my walk through adolescence was a process, and so was my walk with Him. Looking back over my life, I can see the hand of God as I have learned to walk worthy of my calling as a believer in Jesus Christ. I imagine the Apostle Paul was thinking of his friends and co-laborers in Christ as he prayed this prayer for spiritual growth there in the church of Colossae. His faithful prayer was continual. He didn't stop praying for them in their Christian walk and work.

Paul's desire for these believers was that they would walk worthy of the Lord. As we grow and mature in our faith walk, we understand how important our behavior is to God. Through Christ, we can perform good deeds, continue to grow spiritually, and depend on Him for the power we need to endure, persevere, enjoy and express our gratitude to Him for all He has done for us and through us.

Just as it is unthinkable that we would behave the same way now as when we were in junior high school, it is inconceivable that we wouldn't grow in our walk with God. God has called us to walk worthy to further the Gospel of Christ. How do we do this? Through practical obedience and spiritual intelligence, we grow and mature in our faith. As we study the Bible and pray, we become fully equipped by the Holy Spirit at work in our inner being. As we obey God's will in our lives, we bear fruit by getting to know Him better, serving and pleasing Him through our moral excellence. It's not enough to have knowledge but to gain wisdom and understanding so that our character and conduct will reflect the grace of God in our lives. Godly character and conduct come through our spiritual growth and maturity as we yield to God's working power.

Christ reveals our life's purpose as Paul prays for believers to endure with patience, long-suffering, joyfulness, and thanksgiving. Patience in difficult circumstances and self-restraint with all people, especially challenging people. Despite our circumstances, we can be filled with joy and grateful hearts.

We need spiritual intelligence to please God with our lives. Through practical obedience in our walk and work, the Spirit of God will fill us with spiritual power in the inner person. Through that power, it leads to joyful patience and long-suffering with thanksgiving as we claim our inheritance through Christ, qualifying us for our future inheritance in Heaven. AJW

Are you walking worthy of Christ today?

Do others notice a difference in how you face adversity or difficult people?

In what way do you need to mature in patience, long-suffering, joyfulness, or thanksgiving?

Write a prayer of gratefulness to God today and ask Him to help you walk worthy of the call in Christ.

date

scripture

PRAISE & THANKS

PRAYERS FOR MY

CHURCH

FAMILY&FRIENDS

NATION&WORLD

ON MY HEART TODAY

Day 23

Hear and Forgive

---

1 Kings 8:22-53

"And listen to the plea of your servant and of your people Israel,
when they pray toward this place. And listen in heaven your
dwelling place, and when you hear, forgive" (I Kings 8:30, ESV).

Communication is such a big deal. I mean that in a good way. Today,
communication can be used through apps like Zoom (embraced when we
found our culture staying home during the pandemic), FaceTime, FaceBook
Messenger, What's App, or the plethora of other app options that aid us in
communicating with one another in this technology era. We are constantly
learning new ways and the importance of getting our message out in a
way that helps people connect effectively. Interpersonal communication
is still essential for each of us. Without good communication, you cannot
have a healthy marriage or friendship. We are reminded, and we are
constantly challenged to create open and honest communication in our
relationships. But if we are too open and too honest, that may create
its own set of problems for our relationships. That is a topic too big for
our purpose now. However, I think it is essential to understand, and we
cannot overstate, how critical it is to have healthy communication to
promote healthy relationships. Good communication is necessary for our
relationship with God, too.

The prayer we read about in 1 Kings 8 is one of the most extended prayers we will find in our 40-day prayer journey. The wisest man in the Old Testament is perhaps the most long-winded! But there are important lessons for us as we read and observe this dedicatory prayer of the Temple by King Solomon. So, why the topic of communication? Simply stated, King Solomon saw the Temple as a place where God could meet with His people, and they, in turn, could communicate with God. So, the temple was to be a place of prayer.

Note the insights of Solomon as he prayed. First, he acknowledges the covenant relationship God established with his father, King David, the promises that Solomon and the people of Israel enjoyed. The Temple was to be a place of testimony, a reminder to the nation of God's promises. Second, Solomon recognized that the Temple could not contain God. "But will God indeed dwell on the earth? Behold, heaven and the highest heaven cannot contain you; how much less this house that I have built!" (I Kings 8:27, ESV).

The Temple was not a limitation on God but a meeting place for His people to meet with Him. For the Church Age, the New Testament promises to those who trust in Jesus Christ for salvation the presence and indwelling of God's Spirit living in us. Somehow the God who "cannot be contained in the heavens" comes to live within us in a very personal and relational way. According to the Apostle Paul, we are temples of the Holy Spirit. "Or do you not know that your body is a temple of the Holy Spirit within you, whom you have from God? You are not your own, for you were bought with a price. So glorify God in your body" (1 Corinthians 6:19-20, ESV). Our prayers gain power as we recognize that we are praying to the God of Heaven and the Spirit who lives within us. Our bodies become a holy place called a temple, and our prayers are offered as a sacrifice of praise and dedication to our God.

Communication is essential for a healthy relationship. Therefore, the relationship with our Lord Jesus Christ needs to be valued and cultivated by reading His Word, listening to His Spirit, and then talking with Him in prayer.

How does that relate to this prayer of King Solomon? In addition to recognizing the Spirit's indwelling presence, confession is necessary to keep the line of communication open with our Lord. Unconfessed sin leads to an unhealthy relationship. Honest communication is vital for a healthy relationship. Therefore, King Solomon's prayer was one of confession and an expectation of God's forgiveness. "And listen to the plea of your servant and of your people Israel, when they pray toward this place. And listen in heaven your dwelling place, and when you hear, forgive" (I Kings 8:30, ESV).

What often happens to us when we realize that we have done something wrong or, in the same way, been wronged? We want to hide from the person we have wronged or the person who wronged us. We are embarrassed and ashamed and seek to cover up what has occurred. Rather than helping the relationship, it strains and weakens the connection between others and us. Over time, continued wrongs, deceit, and cover-ups will destroy that relationship. I think that is one of the values we can take from King Solomon's prayer. He gives seven different examples of sins that the people of Israel may commit. After listing the scenarios, he asks God to hear their prayers and forgive. Rather than running from God, straining their relationship with Him, the challenge was for the people of Israel to repent and return to the Temple. "Let your eyes be open to the plea of your servant and to the plea of your people Israel, giving ear to them whenever they call to you" (1 Kings 8:52, ESV).

So it is for us. God desires us to run to Him and ask for forgiveness with an open and repentant heart. May I boldly suggest that God wants us to be raw enough to tell Him precisely what we have done wrong rather than asking for forgiveness of sins in general. The Lord's Prayer is a valuable guide to us, encouraging the habit of asking for forgiveness of our sins and trespasses as we forgive others. Anytime we can come to grips with the details of our sins and acknowledge this to God, we gain power in our prayers and intimacy in our relationship with God the Father, Son, and Holy Spirit.

Perhaps the Apostle Paul's concern for grieving the Holy Spirit of God is relevant to this conversation. We cannot allow the Holy Spirit to be uneasy in our lives, unable to dwell with us in peace. "And do not grieve the Holy Spirit of God, by whom you were sealed for the day of redemption" (Ephesians 4:30, ESV). Honest confession and conversation with our Heavenly Father is powerful, praying, and empowers us to enjoy and deepen our relationship with him! MPD

date *scripture*

PRAISE & THANKS

PRAYERS FOR MY

CHURCH

FAMILY&FRIENDS

NATION&WORLD

ON MY HEART TODAY

Day 24

Lord, You Kept Your Promise

---

2 Chronicles 1:7-12

"Give me now wisdom and knowledge to go out and come
in before this people, for who can govern this people of
yours, which is so great?" (2 Chronicles 1:10, ESV).

I was discussing a church project with a friend and explaining that I wished
I was more competent in overcoming some challenges. He responded that
God would give us bigger brains if that were all needed. His point was God
has to accomplish the work, and we need the wisdom to follow what God
is doing. The Book of James encourages us to ask for wisdom. "If any of
you lacks wisdom, let him ask God, who gives generously to all without
reproach, and it will be given him" (James 1:5, ESV). King Solomon
understood the need for wisdom, and this prayer focused on his desire for
wisdom to lead the nation of Israel.

Solomon's prayer begins with acknowledging God's promises to his
father, David, and that he is now sitting as the king because God placed
him there. I wonder, in addition to giving God honor for the covenant
promises to King David and, now, his place in fulfilling the promise if
Solomon felt the weight of kingdom rule in a way that brought him to
recognize how inadequate he was in his knowledge. Solomon's humility
is an example for us. Specifically, he acknowledges God's hand in placing

him on the throne and that he needed the help of God to be successful as king.

God allowed Solomon to ask for anything. While you and I may not think we are in a prominent position of authority or influence, we are invited to come to Him and ask anything as children of the Heavenly Father. But, of course, Jesus reminds us that we must ask in His name. We, like Solomon can ask for anything but is guided to what aligns with God's will and purposes. The words of Jesus are critical for us to learn as we develop our prayer life. "But seek first the kingdom of God and his righteousness, and all these things will be added to you." (Matthew 6:33, ESV). Our prayers mature and gain power as we submit ourselves to the kingdom of God as our first and highest priority.

Solomon chooses wisely by asking God to give him understanding to lead and care for his people. He would not serve as a warrior king like his father but as a builder of the nation of Israel. His gift to the people of Israel was to guide them in such a way that they would flourish. He was also granted the ability to discern between good and evil, and it is fair to say that he was given a common sense that brought practical goodness to the people of Israel. I have had the privilege of interacting with many governing leaders and praying over them. When asked how we should pray for them, the answer is very often, "I need wisdom." I have been tempted to think that is simply a pat answer. But I accept that they genuinely feel the weight of making decisions that will bless the people they serve and create good for them. As the Apostle Paul encourages us to pray for our governing leaders, we should see the opportunity to ask God to grant them wisdom so the people of our state and nation may flourish.

God responds to Solomon with delight and promises to grant him wisdom. Certainly, the Old Testament demonstrates the respect Solomon's wisdom gained for him. The Book of Proverbs is a great example that demonstrates the wisdom God granted to Solomon. Additionally, God promised wealth and riches to Solomon as an added blessing because of his wise choice and concern for others. This brings us back again to the promise of our Lord Jesus Christ that our Heavenly Father will provide all the other necessities of life if we seek God's kingdom. We learn the power of prayer as we forsake selfishness and ask our Heavenly Father to help us see His Kingdom priorities. Our prayers will also be powerful as we imitate King Solomon with a posture of humility. "Do nothing from selfish ambition or conceit, but in humility count others more significant than yourselves. Let each of you look not only to his own interests, but also to the interests of others" (Philippians 2:3-4, ESV). Lord Jesus, help me to seek Your Kingdom first and also to learn to put the interests of others before mine. I humbly offer my thanksgiving to You acknowledging that all that I am as Your child comes by faith in Jesus, and because of Your gracious gifts to me. MPD

date *scripture*

PRAISE & THANKS

PRAYERS FOR MY

CHURCH

FAMILY&FRIENDS

NATION&WORLD

ON MY HEART TODAY

Day 25

Give Success to Your Servant

Nehemiah 1:4-11

"Give Your servant success today, and have compassion on
him in the presence of this man." Nehemiah 1:11 HCSB

On September 11, 2001, Evil breached our nation catastrophically,
jeopardizing the country's very integrity. Rubble and ruin were evidenced
in graphic pictures, videos, and articles breaking the very heart of America.
Our nation mourned in stunned disbelief. Years later, we can now visit
the areas that once had been destroyed. These areas are memorialized with
distinguishing plaques and monuments. Buildings have since been rebuilt.
Life continues around these areas, but no one can argue how life-changing
this event was in the United States.

Israel's remnant had been back in their land for nearly a century. While
the rest had been allowed to leave their Persian captors, many individuals
remained in their new homes. Nehemiah, a cup-bearer to King Artaxerxes,
had remained in the palace in Persia, serving as God had called him to do.
His prominent position put him into a relatively intimate relationship with
the King. He had a grave responsibility in making sure King Artaxerxes
wasn't poisoned but had the privilege of being influential in the day-to-day
running of the kingdom.

However, while Nehemiah was physically present in Persia, his heart
longed to return home to Israel. He cared deeply for his homeland, its

holy city, Jerusalem, and, more importantly, the temple. The place where a nation worshipped together the God of Abraham, Isaac, and Jacob. When his brother, Hanani, arrived back in the Persian empire, Nehemiah wanted to know how the city and temple were coming along. The news was devastatingly brief: "the remnant who survived were in great trouble and disgraced, and Jerusalem lay in ruin."

Nehemiah immediately sat down and wept. After mourning for several days, fasting, and praying, he fell on his face before the God of Heaven, pouring out his heart to confess the nation's sins. Nehemiah's intercessory prayer reminded the nation of Israel of its waywardness in its disobedience. It also reminded a covenant-keeping God that He would bring them home if they repented.

Nehemiah's prayer of confession acknowledges that the nation's sin had brought about its adversities. It was only through God's abundant mercy they survived their captivity. Nehemiah's prayer was also a prayer for God to have compassion for His people, to do what He said He would do, and to restore them to the land God gave them. Finally, Nehemiah prayed boldly for success as he humbled himself before King Artaxerxes to request time to return home to Jerusalem to rebuild the temple, the city, and the wall.

May we follow Nehemiah's example and humble ourselves to pray for our nation and state. Set aside time to fast and pray in earnestness.

Father, we confess the sins committed against You in our country. We pray for a nation to repent of its corruption. Reconcile us to you because you are a Covenant-Keeping God. For those that know and follow Your commands, statutes, and ordinances, may we stay focused on the task You've called us to and give us success in all we do in Your name. Amen. AJW

date

scripture

PRAISE &THANKS

PRAYERS FOR MY

CHURCH

FAMILY&FRIENDS

NATION&WORLD

ON MY **HEART** TODAY

Day 26

Praise for Making Known the King's Matter

Daniel 2:20-23

"May the name of God be praised forever and ever, for wisdom and power belong to Him." Daniel 2:20 HCSB

I have a group of friends called my "Prayer Warriors." When I face a crisis and need wisdom in handling it, I reach out to these warriors and ask them to pray for me. I often believe that God has rewarded our faithful prayers with answered prayers and crisis averted. When this happens, we tend to remind each other of a hymn or praise song related to the situation.

Recently, I had a crisis that involved one of my children. Since she lives 23 hours away from me, I had to rely entirely on faith that God would intervene on her behalf. An S.O.S. went out to my prayer warriors, and immediately, we began to pray individually and collectively. Then, in times of intense praying, God brings to mind the verse, "The effective, fervent prayer of a righteous man avails much" James 5:16 NKJV. The conclusion of this incident brought about much rejoicing, and our daughter's crisis was resolved.

Daniel had surrounded himself with three godly young men. When a life-and-death crisis arose, Daniel immediately contacted these three men and urged them to ask God for mercy concerning the mystery of the king.

Death was imminent without the intervention of Daniel and his praying friends. Now that's a crisis!

Sometime during the night, God revealed the mystery of the king's dream to Daniel. Daniel praised God, offering a song of praise over God's sovereignty and revelation of the deep and hidden things. Because God revealed the mystery to Daniel, He saved Daniel and his friends and delivered the Babylonian wise men and soothsayers.

Although Daniel received the answer, he included his three prayer warriors in the song of praise, "And now You have let me know what we asked of You, for You have let us know the king's mystery." Later in this chapter, Daniel includes his three friends to King Nebuchadnezzar. At Daniel's request, the king also honored his friends by appointing them to the highest office in Babylon.

When we face a crisis in our own lives, we may follow Daniel's example, immediately taking the problem to God through prayer. Others are watching how we handle these moments if we truly live a life of faith in God. Faith rests in the answers of God regardless of the solution. Faith is living in the reality of what we hope and can't see. Whatever the outcome, we can rejoice with those who have helped carry the burden of crisis with us in prayer.

"Whatever God can do, faith can do," said A.W. Tozer, "and whatever faith can do, prayer can do when it is offered in faith."1 Therefore, an invitation to prayer is an invitation to omnipotence, for prayer engages the Omnipotent God and brings Him into our human affairs. AJW

date

scripture

PRAISE & THANKS

PRAYERS FOR MY

CHURCH

FAMILY&FRIENDS

NATION&WORLD

ON MY HEART TODAY

Day 27

Rejoice in the God of My Salvation

1 Samuel 2:1-10

"My heart exults in the LORD; my horn is exalted in
the LORD. My mouth derides my enemies, because I
rejoice in your salvation" (1 Samuel 2:1, ESV).

My wife and I experienced difficulties in having children. We took it for
granted that when we wanted to start a family, we would not have any
problems. But we did! We embarked on all kinds of tests, embarrassing
tests, and eventually, some surgical procedures. As he was visiting with
us about the upcoming procedure he recommended, even one of the
specialists stated that the medical world knows a lot about fertility. Still,
they cannot fully explain how life begins and how the conception process is
accomplished. Granted, that was over thirty years ago, but I think his point
is still valid. Conception and life contain mysteries, ultimately miraculous
gifts from God.

In today's Bible passage, we are introduced to a beautiful prayer of
adoration from Hannah, the mother of Samuel. Hannah's prayer reminds
me of Mary, the mother of Jesus, who prayed and sang her "Magnificat"
when she learned that she would be the mother of our Lord Jesus, as
recorded in Luke 1:46-55. Before looking at the specifics of Hannah's
prayer, we need context. Hannah was unable to bear children. 1 Samuel
1 tells us, "the LORD had closed her womb" (v.5, ESV). Additionally,

Hannah was one of two wives to Elkanah, and she was treated mercilessly by the other wife. "And her rival used to provoke her grievously to irritate her because the LORD had closed her womb" (v. 6, ESV).

Before we arrive at the prayer in 1 Samuel 2, we also need to observe the prayer coming from Hannah's broken heart in chapter 1. You can feel her pain when it is stated, "She was deeply distressed and prayed to the LORD and wept bitterly. And she vowed a vow and said, "O LORD of hosts, if you will indeed look on the affliction of your servant and remember me and not forget your servant, but will give to your servant a son, then I will give him to the LORD all the days of his life, and no razor shall touch his head" (1 Samuel 1:11, ESV).

Some of life's greatest sorrows relate to having or not having children. The feelings of a woman God created with the capacity to bear children is not something a man would carefully dare to address. But I know as a man, I was disappointed and hurt during our journeys to try having children. I say "journeys" because we have two sons, but both times we had difficulties with conception. God graciously gifted us both times, and we celebrate our two sons! Whether the medical procedures cured the problem, we will never know. But we know that children are gifts from God, and our two sons are most definitely gifts from God!

I hope my reflections do not seem like I dwell too long on our experiences. But I want to point out that birth and all its related issues are some of life's most challenging experiences. Some cannot have children; some experience unwanted or unplanned pregnancies; some face children born with physical defects; and some experience miscarriages or the loss of a baby. These are heart-wrenching and very personal realities for many. Realities that must drive us to the throne of grace. "Let us then with confidence draw near to the throne of grace, that we may receive mercy and find grace to help in time of need" (Hebrews 4:16, ESV). Whether having children or any of our other myriads of trials, we can learn from the prayer and experience of Hannah to take the deepest aches and desires of our hearts to the Lord. This is understanding the power of prayer!

I may need to address one other issue before we briefly approach Hannah's prayer in 1 Samuel 2. This Journal looks at the prayers of people in positions of power. Some may conclude that Hannah was a little-known person who desired to have children and was not really in a position of power. Allow me to argue that, as a mom, she was in one of the most powerful positions ever. And as a dad, I would also say that a dad has power in a child's life. Parents hold potent positions over their children. Children can be tortured for life by abusive or even inadequate and lazy parents. Children can also be inspired and directed to great success by loving and caring parents. While never perfect, parents should aspire to be the best parents possible to give their children the best environment to grow and succeed. This brings us again to the importance of prayer. We must ask God to give us wisdom and patience; to provide for our children's needs; and to help us "bring them up in the discipline and instruction of the Lord" (Ephesians 6:4, ESV). Additionally, we should be encouraged to pray for our children to come to saving faith in the Lord Jesus Christ and a life of following their Lord faithfully; for success in their life's journey according to God's plan for them; and for God to bring the right person to be their spouse, if and when they desire marriage.

Almost as a post-script for today, I want to address Hannah's prayer in 1 Samuel 2. It barely references children and motherhood. Instead, it is focused on God's salvation and His Sovereign presence in history. He is holy, all-knowing, all-powerful, and the Judge of all the Earth. He raises people to places of power, wealth, and prestige. He also does the opposite. But God is the only One we can trust for our lives. Whether desiring children or anything else or desiring to find our true purpose in life, the Lord God is the only God of salvation and the only God in Whom we must place our trust. Do not overlook the details of Hannah's child in 1 Samuel 1. She gave her son to the Lord so that he was not even raised in her home. Her satisfaction was found in God's gift and her choice to return His gift to her Lord. Hannah's prayer concludes: "He will guard the feet of his faithful ones, but the wicked shall be cut off in darkness, for not by might shall a man prevail" (1 Samuel 2:9, ESV). Whatever our needs may be now, our ultimate need is to find the God who delights in guarding us and helping us to prevail! Learning to fashion our prayers in line with God's delight is powerful praying! MPD

date *scripture*

PRAISE & THANKS

PRAYERS FOR MY

CHURCH

FAMILY&FRIENDS

NATION&WORLD

ON MY HEART TODAY

Day 28

Our Eyes Are on God

---

2 Chronicles 20:1-30

"O our God, will you not execute judgment on them? For we are powerless against this great horde that is coming against us. We do not know what to do, but our eyes are on you" (2 Chronicles 20:12, ESV).

Many years ago, my wife and I had the opportunity to direct a children's musical about King Jehoshaphat. "Fat, Fat, Jehoshaphat" is a children's musical created by Kathie Hill. I love how the memories of this story have stayed with me over the years. It was my first opportunity to direct a children's musical. Beyond that experience, the message of Jehoshaphat was put into my mind and heart. Jehoshaphat learned the importance of trusting God to deliver him and the nation of Judah through prayer and fasting. He started as "Fat, Fat, Jehoshaphat." and became "Flat, Flat, Jehoshaphat." The author of the musical says, "Fat, Fat Jehoshaphat teaches kids the importance of prayer when faced with any problem." (https://www.kathiehillmusic.com/index.php?main_page=index&cPath=1_144).

So, too, I learned from King Jehoshaphat the importance of prayer. For children and adults, the lesson of facing our problems with prayer and praise is powerful and essential. We may know better, but we often fret and stew and try to do everything in our efforts. Then, as a last resort, we decide that we should pray. Learning to pray first is essential! Pray first, pray throughout, and pray afterward. God may lead us to take action after we pray, but how better to be under the Lord God's direction and have His strength to meet the problem instead of taking action in our strength and without His leading.

Jehoshaphat learned this first principle of prayer very well. The Ammonites and Moabites and Meunites were coming to invade Judah. "Then Jehoshaphat was afraid and set his face to seek the LORD, and proclaimed a fast throughout all Judah (2 Chronicles 20:3, ESV). Cry out to God first. Then, trust Him with our fears and pain, and look for His salvation. The "fat" Jehoshaphat led the people of Judah to fast and pray. According to the children's musical, he became "flat." Jehoshaphat because he fasted. Fasting is a spiritual discipline that is a bigger subject than I can adequately address now. The Church has taken various views on this practice of fasting, but it is worthy of consideration and endorsed by many Scripture references. We were introduced to Nehemiah on Day 25. He is an example of prayer and fasting. "As soon as I heard these words, I sat down and wept and mourned for days, and I continued fasting and praying before the God of heaven" (Nehemiah 1:4, ESV). Those with health issues should use caution and consult medical advice, but fasting allows us to deny our cravings and desires and fully devote our attention to God. I encourage people to seek guidance from their pastor or spiritual mentors on ways to practice fasting and prayer.

King Jehoshaphat's prayer focused on God's covenant with Abraham to faithfully protect His descendants. "Did you not, our God, drive out the inhabitants of this land before your people Israel, and give it forever to the descendants of Abraham, your friend? 8 And they have lived in it and have built for you in it a sanctuary for your name, saying, 'If disaster comes upon us, the sword, judgment, or pestilence, or famine, we will stand before this house and before you —for your name is in this house—and cry out to you in our affliction, and you will hear and save'" (2 Chronicles 20:7-9, ESV). Because God makes and keeps His promises and covenants, our prayers can be supported by faith that God will keep His word. We should remind God of His promises, but we must even more so remind ourselves of His promises, so our prayers become confident statements of trust in God.

Another important character in this story shows up to communicate an endorsement from the Lord God supports King Jehoshaphat and the people of Judah. The prophet, Jahaziel, tells them that they do not need to be afraid and they do not need to do anything. God will fight the battle for them. Sometimes, doing nothing is the hardest thing to do; sometimes, that is precisely what God wants us to do. We learn the power of prayer as we choose to wait on the Lord and, by our prayers, ask Him to go to battle for us. "You will not need to fight in this battle. Stand firm, hold your position, and see the salvation of the LORD on your behalf, O Judah and Jerusalem.' Do not be afraid, and do not be dismayed. Tomorrow go out against them, and the LORD will be with you" (2 Chronicles 20:17, ESV).

One of the hardest lessons to learn in following our Lord is to allow Him to execute vengeance and for us to adopt His grace and patience. The Apostle Paul reminds us how important it is to overcome evil with good. "Beloved, never avenge yourselves, but leave it to the wrath of God, for it is written, 'Vengeance is mine, I will repay, says the Lord.' To the contrary, 'if your enemy is hungry, feed him; if he is thirsty, give him something to drink; for by so doing you will heap burning coals on his head.' Do not be overcome by evil, but overcome evil with good" (Romans 12:19-21, ESV). A powerful prayer is to request our Lord to help us overcome evil with good and to trust God alone to execute justice.

The result of King Jehoshaphat's prayer of faith? The morning of the battle, the people of Judah went out to meet their enemies. The King finally instructed them, "Hear me, Judah and inhabitants of Jerusalem! Believe in the LORD your God, and you will be established; believe his prophets, and you will succeed." (2 Chronicles 20:20, ESV). Don't miss what God did! The Ammonites and the Moabites started fighting the Meunites. The writer of the story says, "they all helped to destroy one another" (2 Chronicles 20:23, ESV).

From this King of Judah, we learn the power of prayer that keeps our focus on our Great and Mighty God. "We do not know what to do, but our eyes are on you." (2 Chronicles 20:12, ESV). MPD

date

scripture

PRAISE & THANKS

PRAYERS FOR MY

CHURCH

FAMILY&FRIENDS

NATION&WORLD

ON MY **HEART TODAY**

Day 29

Search Me, O God!

Psalm 139:1-24

"Search me, God, and know my heart; test me and know
my concerns. See if there is any offensive way in me; lead
me in the everlasting way." Psalm 139:23-24 HCSB

"Search me!" my younger brother would shout as I would accuse him of
taking something of mine. "Fine, I will!" I would declare, trying to chase
him through the house. "Search me" became a catchphrase for many years
in our household. Sometimes it was said with a shrug of the shoulders;
other times, it was said playfully, indicating that some innocent crime had
been perpetrated and an object hidden, waiting to be revealed.

King David's psalm extolling the attributes of God, ends with a bold
prayer for God to "search his heart." It wasn't a childish game of "search
me" but rather a deep, almost painful, desire for God to dig deep into
David's heart and reveal unconfessed sins or offensive ways in him. From
boyhood on, the reader of the Old Testament watches David grow from a
child to the King of Israel.

Early in his youth, David grasped the "bigness" of God as he confronted
Goliath, killed a bear and a lion with his bare hands, and later served under
King Saul. David had the proper knowledge of the God of Israel and knew
it was vital to a fulfilled life here on earth. Perhaps the first part of chapter
139 was David's remembrance of his sin with Bathsheba. Although he

thought his adultery was accomplished in secret, God revealed through the prophet Nathan that David's sin was known in full to the God he served (2 Samuel 11). This intimate relationship between God and His faithful followers prevents us from deceiving ourselves when we submit our thoughts and actions to an omniscient, all-knowing God for His scrutiny.

It would benefit us greatly in our walk with God if we got honest with Him asking Him to "Search Me!" as my brother would say. This kind of search penetrates beyond the facade we live with daily to a digging deeper examination that can sometimes subject us to pain that can lead to healing. When we understand that God knows us intimately and exhaustively, we can rest in the assurance that He knows what is best for us and does all He can for us to make sure that we follow Him as He gently (and sometimes, not so gently) guides and leads us through this life.

God is the only Righteous Judge. He alone can discern our thoughts and actions, revealing to us the actual condition of our hearts. Jeremiah 17:9 reminds us that our hearts are "more deceitful than anything else and incurable," Our heart is beyond cure. Yet, in His love and compassion, the Lord provided a way for our hearts to be forgiven through the gift of His Son, Jesus Christ. Through Jesus' death, burial and resurrection, believers are given a great gift of forgiveness for all the wrong decisions, bad words, hateful thoughts, and prideful actions we've ever done and ever will do.

Let us take time to spend asking God to "search our hearts." When we open the Word of God and allow the Spirit to search us and speak for us, it is then that we will discover the truth about our inward being. We must never dispute with this Righteous Judge. His love for us is incontrovertible and immeasurable. Through this immense love, He will then lead us in the everlasting way of abundant joy and eternal pleasures (Psalm 16:11). AJW

date

scripture

PRAISE & THANKS

PRAYERS FOR MY

CHURCH

FAMILY&FRIENDS

NATION&WORLD

ON MY HEART TODAY

Day 30

Justice is Perverted

Habakkuk 1:2-4

"For the wicked restrict the righteous; therefore, justice
comes out perverted." Habakkuk 1:4b HCSB

"It's just not fair!" I wailed in lament.

"Life's not often fair," my dad would console, 'that's why we trust God's promises. He is just and is the final judge. He knows the score and keeps excellent records."

Have you ever wondered why God seems indifferent to injustice, exploitation, and crooked leaders? Perhaps you've suffered in one of these ways. What was your reaction? How did you respond to God's lack of response to you?

Habakkuk, priest, and prophet to the deteriorating nation of Judah, felt deeply about the injustice of his country. The problem was a collapse of the infrastructure of the leaders who chose not to obey the law, leading to national moral decay. Habakkuk's usage of such strong language in this chapter brought to light just how terrible life was like: violence, iniquity, grievance (or misery), spoiling (or destruction), strife, contention (or disputes), and judicial injustice. Habakkuk was overwhelmed by the degradation of this society and began to lament directly to God.

We, in our society, tend to back away from the excessive expression of grief as a whole. Scripture records several laments of great men of faith, such as Job (Job 3) and Jeremiah (Jer. 11:15-16), King David (Psalm 22:1), and even Jesus (Matt. 27:46). Each of these men of faith lamented God's silence to their pleas to hear them. Their prayers asked for relief from their present circumstances and for God to correct their wrongs. So "where are you, God?" "Why aren't You listening to Your servant?" We are free to bring our laments directly to the Lord, trusting Him fully; even when we don't see His hand moving, we can still trust His promises. Habakkuk's understanding of God's words is another reason why it's so important that we know scripture and hide it away in our hearts (Psalm 119:105). When life is dark, God's Word is our light to guide us.

It seems like the wicked continue to prevail, and justice is perverted. Crying out with boldness before God, Habakkuk points out the nation's wickedness and disbelief that God will use an ungodly nation to bring discipline to rebellious Judah. But God has a plan and will respond to Habakkuk, allowing him time to finish his prayer of lament. Isn't that a comfort to us? Knowing God allows us time to come before Him, praying and lamenting. When we have exhausted ourselves before Him, we can rest assured that He will answer. Perhaps Habakkuk was reflecting on Psalm 46:10, and when his prayer ended, taking time to "be still" in the presence of God. AJW

Have you experienced a time of lament? How did God work in your heart?

Is there a cause or injustice you need to bring before the Lord?

Take time to write it down, pray it out, and wait for the Lord to respond.

date

scripture

PRAISE & THANKS

PRAYERS FOR MY

CHURCH

FAMILY&FRIENDS

NATION&WORLD

ON MY HEART TODAY

Day 31

Joy in the God of My Salvation

Habakkuk 3:1-19

"Yet I will triumph in Yahweh; I will rejoice in the God
of my salvation. Yahweh, my Lord is my strength; He
makes my feet like those of a deer and enables me to walk
on mountain heights!" Habakkuk 3: 18-19 HCSB

In the previous devotional, Habakkuk questioned God, "Where are You,
Lord?" lamenting perverted justice. He cried out to God with honest and
humble questions, wrestling with the fact that God was about to use a
pagan nation to discipline the people of Judah. Have you been there?
Grappling with injustice, why is God not doing something about it? Well,
I have.

Several years ago, my family found itself in a series of calamities that
didn't seem to affect other people. Within six months, my mom passed
away from a long battle with cancer; we moved to a city I had no desire
to move to. Our home didn't sell for over two years, so we moved into the
smallest apartment we could afford, only to be flooded out and lose most
of our worldly possessions. I watched as the waters flowed into our little
abode, helpless and somewhat hopeless. So I began a season of laments
before my God.

I cried until the tears ran dry. Exhausted in my grief, I sat in silence.
God began reminding me of His faithfulness throughout my walk with

Him. Repeatedly, God reminded me how He continued to grow my faith, providing for our needs. God can bring us out of the valley to the mountaintop of worship in moments of trial.

Habakkuk had honestly questioned God, stopping to pray and supplicate before the Holy One. Then he waited on God. We must never rush time with God. He isn't a "fast-food" God but a deliberate, intentional King who deserves our awe and reverence. Like me, Habakkuk couldn't change his circumstances, but by allowing God's preeminence in our lives, God changed our perspective on the work He would perform. In this, Habakkuk penned, "the just shall live by faith" (Hab. 2:4). Walking by faith, not by sight, allows us to intimately experience the majesty and power of our Omnipotent Father God.

Through this prayer, Habakkuk is reminding himself and God of God's past greatness, knowing that this God, who can never change, will continue to prove Himself great. Beginning with the exodus of Egypt, Habakkuk's prayer led to the judgment of the Babylonian captivity, hope in past deliverance, and future hope of the redemption of Judah.

Christians are encouraged to come with confidence before the throne of grace. Circumstances that leave us anxious and afraid can be brought to the feet of Jesus. We can bring our honest laments to our Father in Heaven, waiting on Him to work out His will and purpose in our lives and the world around us. As we walk through the valley, may we rejoice in the truth of Habakkuk's prayerful conclusion "I will rejoice in the God of my salvation!" AJW

Reflection--Have you experienced the crushing blow of calamity? What was your response?

Were you a "worrier" or a "worshipper"?

Spend a few minutes praying, reflecting on how your attitude affects your adoration of the "God of my salvation!"

date

scripture

PRAISE
&THANKS

PRAYERS FOR MY

CHURCH

FAMILY&FRIENDS

NATION&WORLD

ON MY HEART TODAY

Day 32

The Lord is God

---

1 Kings 18:20-40

"Answer me, O LORD, answer me, that this people may
know that you, O LORD, are God, and that you have
turned their hearts back" (1 Kings 18:37, ESV).

The Gunfight at the O.K. Corral movie highlights the showdown between the good and bad guys with a promise of a good fight and the hopes of the good guys winning the battle. Many of us find that a good story that brings the good and the bad to a showdown is an excellent drama worthy of our time and attention. But, of course, the good guys must win! Elijah is presented in our Bible passage as the good guy on the side of Jehovah God. God leads him to face the prophets of Baal, the bad guys promoting the worship of false gods in the land of Israel. The Bible often asks people to choose whether their allegiance is to God or other idols, whether false gods or our desires.

Joshua is one of many examples of a leader who challenged the people of Israel as they prepared to enter the Promised Land to leave behind their false gods and choose to follow Jehovah. "Now, therefore, fear the LORD and serve him in sincerity and faithfulness. Put away the gods that your fathers served beyond the River and in Egypt, and serve the LORD. And if it is evil in your eyes to serve the LORD, choose this day whom you will serve, whether the gods your fathers served in the region beyond the River or the gods of the Amorites in whose land you dwell. But as for me and my house, we will serve the LORD" (Joshua 24:14-15, ESV). Years later, Elijah challenges the people in this public showdown to choose between serving the true God or the false gods.

The showdown is on Mt. Carmel, a test proposed by Elijah to the prophets of Baal. Each side would prepare a sacrifice, and the deity who responds with fire will be the true deity worthy of worship. Elijah gives the prophets of Baal the first opportunity, and they prepare their sacrifice. The location is in their favor; the challenge of fire should be in the expertise of this god Baal, who controls lightning and the weather, and they have the first opportunity to demonstrate the power of Baal. The Scripture writer describes what eventually becomes a foolish but ugly scene. As the day moves from morning to afternoon, the prophets cannot get a response from Baal, and they start to cut and injure themselves, hoping they can somehow tempt their god into a reaction of victory. Interestingly, it is their prayers to a false god that go unanswered. Elijah even underscores these prayers of hopelessness by taunting the prophets. And at noon, Elijah mocked them, saying, "Cry aloud, for he is a god. Either he is musing, relieving himself, or on a journey, or perhaps he is asleep and must be awakened. And they cried aloud and cut themselves after their custom with swords and lances until the blood gushed out upon them. And as midday passed, they raved on until the time of the offering of the oblation, but there was no voice. No one answered; no one paid attention" (I Kings 18:27-29, ESV).

Prayer is a common practice among most of the world's major religions. The question for us to answer is, "To whom are we praying?" The God of Abraham, Isaac, and Jacob is Jehovah God. He is the true God that Elijah represents and calls upon at this great showdown.

Before Elijah prays to Jehovah God, he makes his sacrificial preparation. He uses twelve stones representing the twelve tribes of Israel to build the altar. He places the animal parts appropriately on the altar. Then he asks for a ditch to be dug around the altar and for both the sacrifice and the altar to be drenched in water. Then Elijah offers this prayer: "O LORD, God of Abraham, Isaac, and Israel, let it be known this day that you are God in Israel, that I am your servant, and that I have done all these things at your word. Answer me, O LORD, answer me, that this people may know that you, O LORD, are God and that you have turned their hearts back" (1 Kings 18:36-37, ESV). Jehovah God responds with a fire that consumes the sacrifice, water, altar, and earth. With this glorious display of the good and great power of the true God, the people cry out, "The LORD, he is God; the LORD, he is God" (1 Kings 18:39, ESV).

The prayer of Elijah is brief but powerful. It is a prayer of faith in the true and living God, founded on the revelation of God to Abraham, Isaac, and Jacob. This is the God of the nation of Israel and His glory are now on display. Elijah is interested in something other than showing off or making himself the star. His prayer has this single purpose of demonstrating that the Lord is God. Our prayers become powerful as we seek the true and living God and desire His glory to be displayed. When Jesus issued the Great Commandment, He asked us to represent Him as the true God and the faithful Savior offered to the world. "And Jesus came and said to them, 'All authority in heaven and on earth has been given to me. Go therefore and make disciples of all nations, baptizing them in the name of the Father and of the Son and the Holy Spirit, teaching them to observe all that I have commanded you. And behold, I am with you always, to the end of the age'" (Matthew 28:18-20, ESV). We are challenged to make Him famous and spread the good news! Praying with this purpose empowers us as our Lord is ready and willing to answer these prayers.

So, we pray for opportunities to spread the good news. We pray for people to see the good that God offers to all through Jesus Christ. We pray for the salvation of many people desiring that many would come to know the truth of Jesus as the only Savior of the world. The Apostle Paul guides us toward prayers with this purpose. "First of all, then, I urge that supplications, prayers, intercessions, and thanksgivings be made for all people, for kings and all who are in high positions, that we may lead a peaceful and quiet life, godly and dignified in every way. This is good and pleasing in the sight of God our Savior, who desires all people to be saved and to come to the knowledge of the truth. For there is one God, and there is one mediator between God and men, the man Christ Jesus, who gave himself as a ransom for all, which is the testimony given at the proper time" (1 Timothy 2:1-6, ESV).

These are not simple days where the good and bad guys are distinguished. But the opportunity to call upon Jehovah God for His goodness to be displayed is undoubtedly here. I like how some use the terms "revival" and "awakening". We must be encouraged to pray that our Lord Jesus Christ will revive his Church. Help us as Your Church to not be satisfied with the status quo and not to be nonchalant when it comes to Your testimony as the true God. Wake up your Church, O Lord! Then, awaken the people we live with and interact with each day. Help them see the salvation, glory, and good found only in Jesus Christ! And Lord, help me to represent Jesus and His mighty salvation boldly and humbly, so that through me, others may see and hear about my Lord Jesus Christ! That is powerful praying! MPD date scripture

PRAISE & THANKS

PRAYERS FOR MY

CHURCH

FAMILY&FRIENDS

NATION&WORLD

ON MY HEART TODAY

Day 33

Lord, Help Us See!

---

2 Kings 6:8-23

"Then Elisha prayed and said, 'O LORD, please open
his eyes that he may see" (2 Kings 6:17, ESV).

"Lord, help!" Do you find times when that is the only prayer you can offer?
I wonder if this is a part of what the Apostle Paul had in mind when he
challenged us to "pray without ceasing" (1 Thessalonians 5:18, ESV). I
know that Jesus described the value of having a "Prayer closet." These are
prayer settings when you seek a place and time to secretly talk with God,
whether alone or with a spouse, your children, or a group of friends. Our
Lord Jesus would often pray through the night, and we can learn the value
of this extended and secret prayer. Both types of prayers are necessary tools
for facing the daily challenges of life that cause us to cry out to the Lord for
help. Long sessions of prayer give the advantage of seeking the Lord in an
unhurried and intentional way. Quick prayers of calling out for help give
us a way to seek the Lord immediately to come to our aid. "Lord, help me
say the right words." "Lord, help me represent you well in this situation I
find myself in." "Lord, help me get through the day with patience."

Beyond the many times, we can imagine this cry of help, the one
that may be the most prevalent is "Lord, help me, I am afraid!" Often
fear overcomes us and trumps our faith. When we are fearful, we can
cry for help to the One who reassuringly tells us, "Do not be afraid; I

am with you." We now encounter Elisha and his servant in today's Bible passage. The Syrian king was angry with Elisha in 2 Kings 6 because of Elisha's capacity to impede his military preparations. The Syrian army of horses and chariots was dispatched to Dothan to deal with Elisha to end this annoyance. When Elisha's servant saw this, he was terrified and overwhelmed! I know my response would be fear. Elisha addressed this servant's fear, "Do not be afraid, for those who are with us are more than those who are with them" (2 Kings 6:16, ESV). The Lord God was with Elisha; he knew it, but the servant did not. So, Elisha prayed a prayer of "Lord, help!"

"O LORD, please open his eyes that he may see" (2 Kings 6:17, ESV). Elisha's prayer is incredibly brief compared to many other prayers we have examined throughout this 40-day journey. But it is a fitting prayer to teach us to call on the Lord anytime and anywhere, especially when we are afraid. This prayer is a prayer of empowerment. When we pray, "Lord, help!" or, specifically, in this prayer of Elisha for the ability to see the mighty army of God, it empowers us to know the presence, power, and peace of the Lord our God. God responded affirmatively to Elisha by revealing the heavenly army surrounding them and at the ready to do the Lord's bidding. Similarly, the Apostle John reminds us, "Little children, you are from God and have overcome them, for he who is in you is greater than he who is in the world" (1 John 4:4, ESV).

The Apostle Paul reminds us that following Jesus requires faith and is not dependent on sight. "For we walk by faith, not by sight" (2 Corinthians 5:7, ESV). Our relationship with the Lord Jesus Christ must be a faith relationship. But there are times when we need to know that God is with us. We must see that God is near and ready to calm our spirits. His Holy Spirit, Who is present with us, will assure us that we will not be scared. I believe asking for help is powerful at the moment, and our Lord delights in answering these prayers.

This story of Elisha continues with a humorous conclusion. One more brief prayer from Elisha asks the Lord God to defeat the Syrian army by blinding them. "Please strike this people with blindness" (2 Kings 6:18, ESV). It wasn't the army of Israel that came to defeat this enemy army. Instead, God supernaturally blinded the Syrians, so Elisha and his servant could lead them blindly to Samaria, where the King of Israel could hold them captive. Imagine an army of horses and chariots not being able to see and being led right into the arms of the enemy! I have not had anyone go blind because of my prayers, but God has responded to my prayers for help and provided the comfort and victory I need. When it comes to this spiritual army that Elisha's servant was eventually able to see, we need to remember that there is a spiritual realm beyond what we can see and feel. Around us, in the spiritual sphere, evil and good are engaged in a fierce struggle. But, as the apostle Paul tells us, our Lord Jesus Christ equips us with the spiritual armor and weapons we can use in this spiritual realm. "Put on the whole armor of God, that you may be able to stand against the schemes of the devil. For we do not wrestle against flesh and blood, but against the rulers, against the authorities, against the cosmic powers over this present darkness, against the spiritual forces of evil in the heavenly places. Therefore take up the whole armor of God, that you may be able to withstand in the evil day, and having done all, to stand firm" (Ephesians 6:11-13, ESV). Take the Sword of the Spirit, which is the Bible, as our essential weapon, and then add the second important weapon of "praying at all times in the Spirit, with all prayer and supplication" (Ephesians 6:18, ESV). So how do our prayers become powerful? We stop trusting in our weak selves and see the Word of God and our prayers to God as the way to access the might of our victorious God! MPD

date *scripture*

PRAISE & THANKS

PRAYERS FOR MY

CHURCH

FAMILY&FRIENDS

NATION&WORLD

ON MY HEART TODAY

Day 34

Glorify Your Son

John 17:1-26

"Now, Father, glorify Me in Your presence with the glory I had with You before the world existed." John 17:5 HSCB

In my senior year of high school, I earned the privilege of giving the farewell address at graduation. It seemed like I was the only Christ follower in my school, and I knew I needed to share the gospel message as I gave my speech. Heavily burdened, I fell on my face in prayer. "Father, I don't know why you've allowed me this honor, but please give me the words to say that You will be glorified as I point others to Christ." This simple prayer became my mantra over the weeks leading up to graduation day.

I discovered I had lost my voice on the morning of my graduation. It was barely a squeak. Hiding in my closet, crying, and praying, my mom discovered where I was and said something I will never forget. "God has brought you to a place of great prominence today. He has trusted you with His message of grace and mercy to share with your classmates, their families, and the school's faculty. God has already been honored by you and will glorify you for obeying His call on your life today. Trust me. God will use you powerfully." Then, stepping up to the podium, God strengthened my raspy voice and proclaimed His message. God was glorified by my obedience to honor Him in my speech.

Jesus was preparing to enter a time of great suffering and death on the cross. His mission lay before Him. He was the only way. In a redemptive plan that began before the earth was created, Christ knew He had come to the moment that all humanity would need to save them from an eternity separated from God. In the greatest prayer ever, Jesus gives an account of His earthly ministry as He prepares to fulfill the most crucial mission ever accomplished. Jesus offered Himself as the remission of sin, once and for all, through His great sacrifice on the cross.

Looking up into Heaven, Jesus begins His prayer, asking God to glorify His Son. What a beautiful picture of the deity of Christ! We know that God will not give glory to any other. He does, however, give glory to His Son, who had authority from the beginning. Jesus' mission was complete in His heart, an "already done deal," and as He prayed, He assured the Father that eternal life was now offered to the world. Eternal life comes from a personal relationship of knowing Jesus Christ. The only way to the Father is through the Son. In that, God is exalted, and God glorifies His Son.

Through God glorifying His Son, Jesus is strengthened in His Spirit to sustain the suffering He is about to endure. His sacrifice is the only acceptable remittance of action to save a sinful world. Through the power of God, Jesus will be resurrected, overcoming the power of death and sin, and restored to His pristine glory, sitting down at the right hand of the Father.

Jesus' prayer reminds us that we, as believers, are given an intimate invitation to join in with Christ as He shares all He came to do to bring glory to His Father. Following Christ's mission to bring the good news to others, we bring glory to Him in our obedience. May we come to the end of our lives with the same prayer as Jesus, "I have glorified You on this earth by completing the work You gave Me to do." Fellow believers, we have a mission to complete. Let's do it all for the glory of God! AJW

date *scripture*

PRAISE & THANKS

PRAYERS FOR MY

CHURCH

FAMILY&FRIENDS

NATION&WORLD

ON MY HEART TODAY

Day 35

Sanctify Them in Your Truth

John 17:6-19

"Sanctify them by the truth; Your word is truth. As You have sent Me into the world, I also have sent them into the world. I sanctify Myself for them, so they also may be sanctified by the truth." John 17:18-19 HSCB

This summer, my husband and I became empty-nesters. Our daughters have moved to opposite sides of the United States. We have spent countless hours giving my daughters everything we felt they needed to succeed. Understanding that everyone's journey is different, my husband and I made sure they understood their relationship with Christ is what everything else depends on to be successful.

Jesus knew that His disciples' relationship with Him was what would allow them to be successful in the commission He gave them. The prayer in John 17:6-19 is the second part of Jesus' great prayer. In His intercessory prayer for the disciples, Jesus shares with God the disciples' ministry of what they have begun to do and will continue to do. During his three years with His disciples, Jesus gradually began to reveal God's name, making known the Father's work and words so that He would equip the disciples with wisdom and knowledge. Jesus' compassion towards the disciples is breathtaking. If He were to reveal the power of God's name all at once, they would not have been able to comprehend or endure that kind of experience. In the Old Testament, Moses had requested to see the glory of

God, but that experience would have instantly caused his death. But God, in his graciousness, put Moses in a cleft of a rock and shadowed his glory with his hand so that Moses was able only to see the backside of God's glory. Moses had been set apart, sanctified, and reflected in the glory of God when he entered the Israelite camp. In the same way, the disciples were gifted by God to his son Jesus and sanctified by the truth of the word of God to be spokesmen for Jesus Christ.

Jesus continues to pray for his disciples for their security, joy, and sanctification. Jesus understood what each of them would face by continuing the commission Christ gave them before He ascended into heaven. Revealing Himself to the disciples, the multitudes of people witnessed God's immense power through Jesus. Jesus took the name Jehovah, I AM, and made it powerfully meaningful to His disciples as He walked with them that Jesus is the "I am the bread of life," "I am the light of the world," and "I am the Good Shepherd." By reviewing God the Father's gracious and holy name, Jesus showed the disciples that He was everything they would need when He was no longer with them.

The disciples had been chosen and sanctified by the presence of Jesus, set apart to declare the salvation of the Lord to a world that desperately needed Him and continues to need Him today. God has set apart these men expressly to carry on the Great Commission. Through their relationship with Jesus, they learned that it was not enough just to study scripture and learn doctrinal truth. Their relationship was intimate and personal. A deep and abiding relationship is the encouragement of sanctification, in being set apart for Christ, that we should desire to live. Like the disciples, living a life of obedience, loving Our Savior more each day, and glorifying Him through lives lived as intercessors of the ministry of Christ. AJW

date *scripture*

PRAISE & THANKS

PRAYERS FOR MY

CHURCH

FAMILY&FRIENDS

NATION&WORLD

ON MY HEART TODAY

Day 36

That They May Be One

John 17:20-26

"I am in them, and You are in Me. May they be made
completely one so the world may know You have sent Me and
have loved them as You have loved Me." John 17:23 HSCB

"I have been praying for you before I even met you," my mother-in-law told
me shortly before I married her son. "When I had David, I began praying
for a wife, a help-mate, that would love God, love my son, and become one
as husband and wife." I was moved with emotion but didn't fully grasp
what she was sharing with me until I gave birth to our daughters and began
to pray for their future husbands. I prayed God would bless them with
husbands that had a personal walk with Jesus, loved God, and would, at
the appointed time, become one as husband and wife. I prayed, in both
cases, before our daughters and future sons-in-law were born that they
would eventually become One with Christ and one with my daughters.

Jesus' prayer and vision for future believers transcended the present
moment of His prayer, expressing His concern for His followers to be
"one" in unity and love. This unity would ultimately reflect the indivisible
unity of God the Father, the Son, and the Holy Spirit. This unity would
bear witness to Jesus' identity as the One sent by the Father, the evidence
of the Trinity. Jesus' prayer focuses on the future: for believers today and
the church throughout the ages.

Christ's glory is revealed through the unity of His children and reflected in the person and work of Christ. That same glory that belongs to Christ belongs to believers today. Jesus promised that as we live in unity and love, we will one day experience the future glory of Heaven with Him. This hope draws us to Christ as we work and grow in the gospel ministry. In this maturing and growing, the glory within us rises and reveals itself in what we say and do and the actions accompanying our words. The world should see Jesus' glory reflected through us as we glorify Him in living out the gospel message.

In prayer, Jesus continued to report to the Father about the ministry believers will have in this world and His desire to be equipped through His glory. As believers, our task is to bear witness to the world by sharing the gospel or good news of Christ. However, we must be cautious in presenting the gospel in truth and love. Ephesians 4:15 "But speaking the truth in love, let us grow in every way into Him who is the head-Christ." Theologian Warren Wiersbe stated, "It has well been said that truth without love is brutality, but love without truth is hypocrisy." (The Bible Exposition Commentary, New Testament, Warren Wiersbe, p. 372) If we become puffed up with knowledge, it results in pride. If we exhibit love alone, it can lead to wrong decisions. The Apostle Paul knew this, praying for believers "that love will keep on growing in knowledge and every kind of discernment so that you can approve the things that are superior and can be pure and blameless in the day of Christ.." (Phil. 1:9-10)

May we be able to say, as our Savior did at the end of His earthly ministry, "I have glorified You on the earth by completing the work You gave Me to do" as we finish the task that Jesus prayed for us to do as His representatives to the world. His prayer is still before our Father in Heaven. What an encouragement to know that Christ was praying for us before we were born and that we would share in the "oneness" that He shares with God! AJW

date

scripture

PRAISE
& THANKS

PRAYERS FOR MY

CHURCH

FAMILY&FRIENDS

NATION&WORLD

ON MY HEART TODAY

Day 37

Speak the Word with Boldness

Acts 4:1-31

"And now, Lord, look upon their threats and grant to your servants
to continue to speak your word with all boldness, 30 while you
stretch out your hand to heal, and signs and wonders are performed
through the name of your holy servant Jesus" (Acts 4:29-30, ESV).

Aleksandr Solzhenitsyn, one of the more famous and bold dissidents in the
former Soviet Union, stated:

"Over a half-century ago, while I was still a child, I recall hearing a
number of old people offer the following explanation for the great disasters
that had befallen Russia: "Men have forgotten God; that's why all this has
happened." Since then I have spent well-nigh 50 years working on the
history of our revolution; in the process, I have read hundreds of books,
collected hundreds of personal testimonies and have already contributed
eight volumes of my own toward the effort of clearing away the rubble left
by that upheaval. But if I were asked today to formulate as concisely as
possible the main cause of the ruinous revolution that swallowed up some
60 million of our people, I could not put it more accurately than to repeat:
"Men have forgotten God; that's why all this has happened." (https://www.
goodreads.com/quotes/365427-over-a-half-century-ago-while-i-was-still-a)

His observation is worthy of our attention, but his willingness to do
and say the right thing in the face of persecution by his government is

also worth noting and emulating. He is one example of many through the centuries since our Lord's death and resurrection who have been willing to speak the truth about Jesus Christ boldly. The Book of Acts records the early days of the Apostles and followers of Jesus as they sought to live out their faith in Jesus and spread the good news. In our text, the Church, alongside the Apostle Peter and John, were experiencing the pressure to be silenced and chose instead to be obedient to the message and instruction of their Lord. "But Peter and John answered them, 'Whether it is right in the sight of God to listen to you rather than to God, you must judge, for we cannot but speak of what we have seen and heard'" (Acts 4:19-20, ESV). With enthusiasm and faith, they did not back down and asked God to grant them continued boldness to express this important message. We need to be bold and faithful to present the good news. Our boldness will be acquired through prayer. We must determine to pray this kind of powerful prayer as the early Church in Acts did.

Why should we pray for boldness? Because we will fail in our strength. And we will not be able to accomplish what only God can do. While they prayed for boldness, they expected the Lord to do the miraculous. Their prayers filled the Holy Spirit and spoke God's Word with boldness. Being filled with the Spirit is being directed, controlled, and empowered by Him. The Holy Spirit is delighted to work in and through us to accomplish His work. He will make us bold and effective as we depend on Him. All the good that God wants to accomplish, specifically salvation in our world, is done through the Spirit of God. We are simply asked to be ready to say and do what is right by boldly acknowledging Jesus is Lord and not giving in to the forces who try to dissuade us.

Christians in many places in the world are experiencing persecution for their faith. Recent stories from a pastor in India tell of the persecutions of pastors and Christians because people in the lower caste are finding worth and value beyond their status because they learn that Jesus Christ loves them, and He died for them. Even in the United States, Christians often believe they cannot say anything about their faith in Jesus Christ in the workplace or public schools. Whether officially reprimanded for speaking about their faith or feeling an unspoken pressure to keep silent, we must pray for boldness to speak of our faith in the Lord Jesus Christ and also courage to live a life that backs up our words.

The prayers of the Book of Acts are filled with history. They recite history to understand the tragic situation of our world while God was also doing His marvelous work in history. Why were the authorities so adamantly against the good works and words of the Apostles? The Scriptures taught the Church that the rulers were gathered against the Lord and his Anointed. So, the prayer of the Church in Acts 4 rehearsed the words of King David and reviewed the journey of their Lord as He was taken to the cross to die in our place.

"And when they heard it, they lifted their voices together to God and said, 'Sovereign Lord, who made the heaven and the earth and the sea and everything in them, who through the mouth of our father David, your servant, said by the Holy Spirit, "Why did the Gentiles rage, and the people plot in vain? The kings of the earth set themselves, and the rulers were gathered together, against the Lord and against his Anointed'—for truly in this city, there were gathered together against your holy servant Jesus, whom you anointed, both Herod and Pontius Pilate, along with the Gentiles and the peoples of Israel, to do whatever your hand and your plan had predestined to take place" (Acts 4:24-28, ESV).

They recited Scripture to God in their prayer. Our prayers become powerful as we learn and memorize Scripture and then repeat it to God in our prayers. Prayer makes us bold! We will find the strength not to back down but to be brave and to do what is right. Representing Jesus and His salvation is a privilege, and we must be ready when the world doesn't want to hear or see the joy we have in knowing Jesus Christ. We face our daily battles in our world with prayer and in prayer. It is a powerful prayer of the Church to ask and see the Holy Spirit fill us, accomplish His mighty work, and make us bold! MPD

date

scripture

PRAISE & THANKS

PRAYERS FOR MY

CHURCH

FAMILY&FRIENDS

NATION&WORLD

ON MY HEART TODAY

Day 38

Please Go With Us!

Exodus 33:12-23

"My presence will go with you, and I will give you rest."

It's lonely at the top. Whether feeling the weight of leadership decisions or finding yourself in pressure moments that others would not understand, I think there is a fair amount of truth in the statement. Moses was challenged to lead the Jewish people out of Egypt and into the Promised Land. He needed to be a strategic leader, but he was also responsible for listening to God and representing Him to the people. Easier said than done! Yes, God proved faithful and more potent than Pharoah as He brought the people safely through the waters and then drowned Pharoah and his army in the Red Sea. But the Israelites were people who acted like, well, people! When the going gets tough, many of us get scared and worried and give up. The Israelites also demonstrated another ugly part of our human nature. When Moses met with God on Mount Sinai and his return was too long, the people gave up on Moses and gave in to their lesser angels. The old nature that rebels against the True and Living God began to work, and the people convinced Aaron to create a golden calf to worship. Their rebellion against God kept the Lord God unable to continue His presence with the people and Moses was left with a problem.

God told Moses that He would protect the people but not dwell with them. In other words, the relationship between God and His people was broken. Moses found himself as a lonely leader with people who did not follow God. Moses knew it was not good. In today's Bible passage, we find him in a prayer conversation that asks the Lord God to return and lead His people. Moses put a line in the sand. He told the Lord God that the people of Israel would not journey forward unless God agreed to dwell among His people and lead them. It was not an impertinent request. It was a request of desperation, and God responded affirmatively.

Our lives are impotent without the presence of God in our lives. Not just a distant presence but an intimate presence. Moses desired the personal presence of God that would lead the people safely to their destination. I know that intimacy may not be a very masculine concept, but male or female, we need intimate and meaningful relationships. And that is true for our relationship with God. Moses continued learning the joy and the necessity for God to be intimately involved in his world. He did not want to lose such a gift and knew he would ultimately fail as a leader if God left him alone. God, I need you! I need you to be with me, to protect me, and to guide me. We learn to pray powerfully when we know our need for God and desire nothing better than Him. We also learn to be better leaders and influencers of people because we draw them into our preferred world of intimate relationship with God.

Moses' prayer takes two more additional steps that we should not overlook. With the promise of God's presence, Moses desires to learn more about God and deepen his relationship with God. The joy of a relationship is getting to know a person better, loving who they are, and enjoying every experience with them. Moses knew that God was righteous and could not tolerate the rebellious sin of the people. But he also knew that he and every Israelite would miss out on the pleasures of being with God and benefitting from His gifts if God left them alone. Moses knew his leadership would be ineffective without God's presence and guidance. I believe his desire mirrors the passion of the Apostle Paul, and this passion will accomplish a deep work in our souls that develops a better and more effective leader. "That I may know him (Christ) and the power of his resurrection, and may share his sufferings, becoming like him in his death, that by any means possible I may attain the resurrection from the dead" (Philippians 3:10, ESV). Lord Jesus, allow me to draw near to you and get to know you more and more. Allow me to experience the promise, "Draw near to God, and he will draw near to you" (James 4:8, ESV) Help me to be like You and to live like You desire me to live. Amen.

One other piece of this conversation is worthy of note. In fact, "worthy" is the key. God alone is worthy. He is glorious, magnificent, and beautiful. Moses asks for another aspect of deepening his relationship with God and the people's relationship with God. "Moses said, 'Please show me your glory'" (Exodus 33:18, ESV). This is so awesome! Moses wants God to be the star. He must be the center of our attention and desire. God loves this request and responds positively. Not that God is an egomaniac or narcissistic. We are sometimes guilty of accusing God of what He cannot do. By his nature, God is glorious, and He knows that sharing His glory with us is good for us. We want our friends and family to share their good qualities with us. Similarly, God is good, and we should be delighted that He is willing to share His glory with us. God agrees to give Moses this special gift. Promising to share His glory, He also reminds Moses of His glorious name. The promise-keeping Lord is merciful, gracious, loving, and ready to forgive. That is the fullness revealed in His name! How can we be in a relationship with God? Through His gracious gift of love and forgiveness. How can we deepen our relationship with God? Through His gracious gift of love and forgiveness. But we also must be warned. No one can take advantage of God. The tendency to return to the gods of Egypt had to be banished from within the Israelites. The same is true for us. God cannot and will not allow our evil tendencies to continue to reign in our lives. His grace and love will eventually say no more. His goodness must take over and rule.

Listening to the earnest prayers of people seeking God and asking for His forgiveness and grace is a delight. Hearing the hearts of people seeking God's glory and asking for the Lord, our God to intervene in our world is effective and powerful in praying. We should be encouraged to ask God to step in and stop our world's ugly and terrible deeds that damage and destroy people. We must ask for a supernatural move of God's Spirit to bring an awakening in our world. Awaken our world to know that God is God alone; He is the true and living God; and He alone gives salvation through the Savior, our Lord Jesus Christ. "And there is salvation in no one else, for there is no other name under heaven given among men by which we must be saved" (Acts 4:12, ESV). MPD

date

scripture

PRAISE
& THANKS

PRAYERS FOR MY

CHURCH

FAMILY&FRIENDS

NATION&WORLD

ON MY HEART TODAY

Day 39

Jesus Glorified in You

---

2 Thessalonians 1:11-13

"We always pray for you that our God will consider you worthy of His calling and will, by His power, fulfill every desire for goodness and the work of faith so that the name of our Lord Jesus will be glorified by you and you by Him, according to the grace of our God and the Lord Jesus Christ." 2 Thess. 1:11-13 HCSB

It had been a year! My mom passed away from a lengthy battle with cancer. My family moved to a new city, but our house sat unsold on the market, so we rented a small lower-level apartment until it sold. Our youngest daughter went from a class of 52 students to over 400 students. Our oldest daughter suffered emotional abuse at work, leaving her unemployed and traumatized. Then to top it all off, the flood of 2018 happened! The intense storm that hit Ankeny that June flooded our lower-level apartment, and we lost all we had, only to be homeless for several weeks until we could find a permanent living arrangement. It took four more months for our house to sell for a substantially lower amount. We were depleted and reeling from so many trials without reprieve.

During this time, God was working on my very self-sufficient attitude. While the trials increased and we were pressed in on every side, God was faithful to provide what we needed when we needed it. And what I needed was a good dose of Him! My journey to the death of "self-sufficiency" finally occurred when, after another round of seemingly endless challenges, I submitted my will to God's will and trusted Him by obediently listening to His small still voice. It was only then that my walk began to glorify Christ. My countenance changed from consternation to peace, my heart shifted from anxiousness to calm, and my prayers changed to gratefulness rather than constant neediness.

Paul's prayer for the believers in Thessalonica was born out of their enduring persecution and affliction, believing the time of Christ's return was imminent. They were struggling, so Paul wanted to remind them to stay faithful to God's calling in their lives, not to give in and grow idle waiting for Christ to come back, but to "keep on keeping on"! Paul's concern was for their worthiness during their present affliction and trials. He reminds them that life's circumstances do not make a person but reveal what a person is truly made of. Through these trials, our faith is tried, and we demonstrate our worth in Christ.

Paul encouraged these believers to stay focused on their walk in Christ. Their character should lead to conduct that pleases God. When we face trials, we can be assured that when we walk in obedience and service to God, He will empower us as our trust in Him increases. We may not fully understand why we have to face some challenges, but we know that all things work for our good and His glory!

Through their worthiness and walk in Christ, their witness is witnessed by the world around them. How often do we forget others are watching to see how we handle situations? I was deeply chagrined when I realized that after one challenging day, my behavior was less than godly; I noticed my children watching me. Immediately, I asked them for forgiveness for my lack of trusting God, and we prayed together for God to be glorified through us in whatever our situation. It's hard to pretend things are great, especially when they aren't, but in the power of the Holy Spirit, we can trust God to strengthen our faith and increase our love for Him and others as we endure each trial and affliction with His supernatural power. Through this, we can take to heart Paul's encouragement in Romans 8:18, "For I consider that the sufferings of this present time are not worth comparing with the glory that is going to be revealed to us." AJW

What is your source of power and strength when you face difficult trials and affliction?

Plug into the power of God through His Word. Take time to pray for an extra measure of faith as you endure the trial through which you walk. Ask God to be glorified in you so you might glorify His Son, Jesus Christ.

date *scripture*

PRAISE & THANKS

PRAYERS FOR MY

CHURCH

FAMILY&FRIENDS

NATION&WORLD

ON MY HEART TODAY

Day 40

Worthy is the Lamb!

Revelation 5:1-14

"Worthy is the Lamb who was slain, to receive power
and wealth and wisdom and might and honor and
glory and blessing!" (Revelation 5:12, ESV)

Seeing the northern lights, the mighty Mississippi, and the Eiffel Tower, watching my bride walk down the aisle, and the births of my two sons; are awe-inspiring moments. They create wonder, joy, and a sense of amazement. Additionally, I will admit that the Lincoln Memorial in Washington, D.C., creates an almost religious experience for me. Seeing the large image of Abraham Lincoln seated on a chair that seems like a throne and the pillars that create a temple-like experience, then reading the solemn words of the Gettysburg Address and his Second Presidential Inaugural Address. Entering this revered memorial is exhilarating and creates a sense of awe within me. However, our earthly and human experiences will pale compared to seeing Heaven and the Throne of God. The Book of the Revelation of Jesus Christ gives a glimpse of the amazing scenes of heaven that await us. Reading the Scriptural descriptions in chapters four and five will create anticipation and that sense of awe and wonder at the majesty of God. Be sure to read today's Bible passage in Revelation 5 and, if you can take the additional time, read chapter four first and then chapter five.

As we focus on Revelation 5, the Apostle John is brought to the heavenly realm to view the scene of the Lamb of God in the company of the Father and Holy Spirit. The Lamb is alone Worthy to take the scroll from the Father. He is eligible, powerful, and capable of taking the scroll and orchestrating the redemption of humanity and the created world because of His sacrifice. "Worthy are you to take the scroll and to open its seals, for you were slain, and by your blood, you ransomed people for God from every tribe and language and people and nation, and you have made them a kingdom and priests to our God, and they shall reign on the earth." (Revelation 5:9-10, ESV).

This is majestic and fascinating, presenting a worship scene around the throne. So, what does this have to do with prayer? Powerful prayers include worship of this glorious God, Father, Son, and Holy Spirit are revealed to us in this heavenly scene. Prayer helps us to see and appreciate our Redeemer, the Lamb of God. "Worthy is the Lamb who was slain." (Revelation 5:12, ESV). Our Redeemer, the Lord Jesus Christ, gives us authority to enter into the presence of our Heavenly Father and offer our prayers with the guidance of the Holy Spirit. The scene of Heaven presented in our Scripture passage inspires hope in us and gives assurance that our Lord will reign forever and that His work of salvation will be completed.

The four living creatures and the twenty-four elders circle the Throne. With harps and bowls of incense, which many believe are the saints' prayers, they bow down in worship before the Throne. Representing the Church, the redeemed people of God stand in awe and celebratory joy of the Lamb who was slain on their behalf.

Jesus, the Lamb of God, is gathering people from every place and nation for His Heavenly Kingdom. He has made us both a Kingdom and Priests to our God. When we worship in prayer, we give honor to the One who is most deserving of it. Prayer draws our hearts to a higher realm that overcomes our defeats, disappointments, sorrows, and cynicism. Worship assures us that our Lord Jesus reigns, and we are on the victory side! Prayer creates an opportunity for us to worship the Lord our God, whether in the calm of the morning before the day gets hectic, in the frantic race to begin the day and get to our destinations on time; in the crunch and pressures of the day; or in the moments before we close our eyes to go to sleep. Anytime and anyplace, we can rehearse the glories of our wonderful Savior, our merciful Heavenly Father and our kind companion, the Holy Spirit. We remember that our God is worthy of worship, and we are carried to the Heavenly realm where God's grace and peace become very real to us in His majestic beauty. This is powerful praying, worship, and victory! MPD

> And I heard every creature in heaven and on earth and under the earth and in the sea, and all that is in them, saying, "To him who sits on the throne and to the Lamb be blessing and honor and glory and might forever and ever!" And the four living creatures said, "Amen!" and the elders fell down and worshiped" (Revelation 5:13-14, ESV).

date *scripture*

PRAISE
& THANKS

PRAYERS FOR MY

CHURCH

FAMILY&FRIENDS

NATION&WORLD

ON MY HEART TODAY

Resources

Holman Christian Standard Study Bible, Copyright 2004, Holman Bible Publishers. Used for all Scripture references

The Bible Knowledge Commentary New Testament, John F. Walvoord & Roy B. Zuck

The Bible Exposition Commentary Old Testament and New Testament, Warren Wiersbe

The Holy Bible, English Standard Version, Copyright 2001, Crossway Publishers, a division of Good News Publishers is used for most Scripture references.

New Living Translation Bible, Copyright 1996, Tyndale House Publishers. Used for Introduction Scripture reference.

Printed in the United States
by Baker & Taylor Publisher Services